WHY SCHOOL COMMUNICATION MATTERS

Strategies from PR Professionals

Kitty Porterfield and Meg Carnes

Published in Partnership with the
American Association of School Administrators

Rowman & Littlefield Education
Lanham • New York • Toronto • Plymouth, UK

Published in Partnership with the American Association of School Administrators

Published in the United States of America
by Rowman & Littlefield Education
A Division of Rowman & Littlefield Publishers, Inc.
A wholly owned subsidary of The Rowman & Littlefield Publishing Group, Inc.
4501 Forbes Boulevard, Suite 200, Lanham, Maryland 20706
www.rowmaneducation.com

Estover Road
Plymouth PL6 7PY
United Kingdom

British Library Cataloguing in Publication Information Available

Library of Congress Cataloging-in-Publication Data

Porterfield, Kitty, 1941–
  Why school communication matters : strategies from PR professionals / Kitty
Porterfield and Meg Carnes.
     p. cm.
  ISBN-13: 978-1-57886-832-2 (cloth : alk. paper)
  ISBN-10: 1-57886-832-7 (cloth : alk. paper)
  ISBN-13: 978-1-57886-833-9 (pbk. : alk. paper)
  ISBN-10: 1-57886-833-5 (pbk. : alk. paper)
  1. School administrators—Professional relationships. 2. Communication in
education. 3. Public relations. I. Carnes, Meg, 1951– II. Title.
  LB2831.8.P67 2008
  371.2—dc22   2008010141

∞™ The paper used in this publication meets the minimum requirements of
American National Standard for Information Sciences—Permanence of Paper
for Printed Library Materials, ANSI/NISO Z39.48-1992.
Manufactured in the United States of America.

For Jovan and Charlie

CONTENTS

Acknowledgments   ix

Foreword   xi

Introduction: A Matter of Urgency   1

PART I   THE RELATIONSHIPS

1   Start with a Win   13
Staying Ahead in a Changing World

2   Build Trust   25
Demonstrating Respect, Competence, and Integrity

3   Win by Persuasion   34
Using Communication to Gain Friends and Influence People

4   Listen to the New Generations   41
Reaching Out to Those Who Expect to Connect

5   Engage the Community   48
Breaking Gridlock

PART II   THE FRAMEWORK

6   Design Your Offense   59
Engaging Stakeholders to Drive Achievement

7   Harness Your Secret Weapon   70
Communicating Effectively with Colleagues and Employees

8   Nail Your Successes   82
Being Accountable in a Data-Driven World

9   Get in the Ring   91
Claiming Our Political Heritage

10   Mind Your Reputation   100
Marketing Your School's (or District's) Greatness

PART III   THE SPECIAL INTERESTS

11   Invest in the Media   113
Protecting Your Assets

12   Lead the Change   124
Modeling a Compelling Message on Diversity

13   Face Those Angry Parents   133
Turning a Complaint into a Gift

14   Dazzle the 80 Percent   145
Reaching Out to the Larger Community

PART IV   THE CRISIS

15   Think Smart under Fire   159
Mastering Basic Crisis Communications

16   A Case Study in Crisis Communications   169
Revisiting Our Assumptions

PART V   THE TOOLBOX

17   Overhaul Daily Communication   181
Creating a Collaborative Culture

18   Read Your School (or District) Newsletter   189
        Understanding Why Parents Don't

19   Manage Your School (or District) Website   195
        Ensuring This Powerful Tool Works for You

20   Get a Grip on Social Media   204
        Playing a Role in Web Conversation

21   Write with Purpose   212
        Harnessing the Punch of the Written Word

22   Upgrade Back-to-School Night   221
        Curing What Ails This Annual Event

Conclusion: Sustainability: The Challenge of the Long-Distance Runner   228

References   236

Index   241

About the Authors   249

ACKNOWLEDGMENTS

No endeavor of this magnitude is ever accomplished alone—or even by two. We have been supported in so many ways by so many friends and colleagues.

First, we must acknowledge the tremendous debt we owe to our former boss, Dr. Daniel Domenech, who was then superintendent of Fairfax County Public Schools. Without his vision and his support we could not have built the network of school-community relationships that the schools in Fairfax County enjoyed and that prompted us to write this book.

We have wonderful friends who read pieces of this manuscript and offered insight along the way. Chief among them were Stephen Hockett, Mary Agnes Garman, Jay McClain, John Porter, Paul Regnier, Jay Mathews, Denny Berry, Teressa Caldwell, and Mel Riddile. Rich Bagin made the resources of the National School Public Relations Association available to us, for which we are grateful. Special thanks to Jill Kurtz for her wisdom and her technological genius.

Other faithful friends offered much-needed expertise and encouragement: Anne Murphy, Ann Monday, Brad Draeger, Barbara Miller, Deborah Bigelow, Rebecca Perry, Steve Gamble, Brigid Schulte, Linda Erdos, Alan Leis, Meredith Wade, Andy Plattner, Brian Edwards, Michelle

Bogre, Ellen Schoetzau, Mike Engley, Larry Byers, Mary Anne Mayer, Judy Christian, Sue Morris, Eileen Kugler, Mary Ann Knox, Lou and Mike Brodecky, and all our colleagues in the Chesapeake Chapter of the National School Public Relations Association.

Our hats are off too to all the wonderful education leaders in Fairfax County Public Schools with whom we had the privilege of working and from whom we learned so much—the leadership team, the principals and assistant principals, and especially all our colleagues in the Office of Community Relations. There never was a better communications team!

We also want to recognize several persons on whose research our work stands and who have been most generous in sharing their time and knowledge with us: Jim and Lauri Grunig, Christine Pearson, Valarie Zeithaml, and Bill Strauss who, sadly, died before we could share this manuscript with him.

Thanks to Joe Cirasuolo and Amy Vogt at American Association of School Administrators for their help and to our editors, Paul Cacciato and Catherine Forrest Getzie.

And finally, our long-suffering families who foraged for their own suppers and listened to all our complaints. We are lucky to have terrific and supportive moms: Kay Burnett and Rita Carnes. Meg's husband Charlie, her brothers John and Jim and their families, and Kitty's kids, Karen, Deborah, and Michael, have edited drafts, scoured websites for information, and brought their own expertise to the project. We miss Jovan a lot.

Foreword
GETTING IT RIGHT

Why Good School Communication Matters

As a superintendent for thirty-two years, I have learned that there are many ingredients for success but one stands out above the rest—great communication skills. You can have the most innovative reform plan around, but if you are not effective in communicating about that plan, it will fail. I have seen good superintendents who do not put a priority on communications forced from their jobs while less deserving superintendents who are better at the art of communications keep theirs. The simple reality of public education today is that superintendents must be outstanding educators *and* they must also be outstanding communicators.

Kitty Porterfield and Meg Carnes articulate this idea very clearly in making the case why exceptional communications skills are so critical for school administrators today. We see example after example of what poor communication practice yields and we see how great communications practices ultimately improve student achievement, which is our common goal. As a group, educators historically have not placed a premium on the importance of good communications. We typically focus on those things we know best—curriculum, professional development, and operations—to name just a few. It is not as if well-intentioned administrators and superintendents have set out to practice ineffective communications. Rather, it happens because communication has not been made a priority, and is often approached only as an add-on or after-thought.

Communications must be approached creatively and strategically. It must be an integral part of the planning of any initiative or effort from the earliest days, not at the end of the process after all of the important decisions are made. Ms. Porterfield and Ms. Carnes provide a great deal of useful advice for practitioners throughout this book to help school districts improve their communications strategy. The old adage that "if you fail to plan, you plan to fail" rings true in every chapter. Ultimately, they drive home the point that if done well, good communications make administrators more effective and stakeholders more satisfied, and increases student achievement.

Like so many other things in life, excellent communications starts with relationships—strong, trusting relationships. You must create and nurture these relationships with your key stakeholder groups, both internal and external. Such relationships are truly the lifeblood for building support for educational reforms or making changes that otherwise might cause significant upset. Doing the right thing for students isn't always the popular thing, and administrators know this better than anyone. Having healthy relationships built on trust can lessen the negative impact of those decisions that may make some of your stakeholders unhappy. A cache of good will makes it possible to create buy in on difficult decisions and assuage those who might otherwise start a wave of protest.

Involve your stakeholders—both internal and external. One of the surest ways to build trust is to open the doors and invite everyone in. Nothing builds trust like transparency. Our stakeholders want to be involved and I believe we all benefit when our stakeholders are part of the process. When we work together and we see that we all want what is best for the children, good things happen. We can use that collective energy to drive student achievement and create a superior learning environment for our students.

The good news is that now there are more communications tools at our disposal than ever before to get the word out. That means we as educators must be nimble and adroit at using new media to effectively communicate with our stakeholders. Whether it is at the school or district level, administrators and superintendents need to recognize the power of the new methods of communication and harness it for positive results. The immediacy of much of the new media world poses difficult challenges for us as well. Good news travels fast, but bad news travels at warp speed. That's why it is critical to build a communications infrastructure to communicate your message and to be prepared to handle other issues that arise.

The bottom line is that creating a healthy environment for positive communications and outstanding student achievement must be part of our daily work. As much as administrators plan and work to ensure that a school is operating smoothly, the busses running on time, the teachers and students have what they need in the classroom, they must also integrate the work of communications in their daily life. In public education today, we need all the support we can get from parents, community and business leaders, elected officials, and others. We build that support through strong communications, by involving everyone in the process and keeping our eyes on the mission at hand—preparing our students for the world ahead. Ms. Porterfield and Ms. Carnes provide many excellent ideas throughout this book about how to make good school communication a reality so that public education continues to work for everyone.

Jerry D. Weast, Ed.D.
Superintendent, Montgomery County Public Schools

Introduction
A MATTER OF URGENCY

Obstacles are the entry point.

—Cyndi Lee

Some years ago, a superintendent of a large, urban school district launched a major initiative to increase the quality of the district's customer service. Research convinced him that offering excellent customer care throughout the organization would improve employee morale and raise the school division's approval rating in the community. The superintendent announced his intention and established a small task force to create a set of standards by which customer service efforts could be measured.

Initially, his plan was met with hefty resistance within the organization.

"What does a school have to do with customer service?" employees grumbled. "Our business is education. Our business is teaching students to read and think. Everyone knows we do a good job!"

Hmmmm. . . . Are we sure about that?

With student test scores being held to high, very public, and sometimes arbitrary standards, with school bond proposals failing in many

communities and budget fights increasingly bitter, with the media running "gotcha" stories about "lax" school building security, with a growing
number of highly organized and vocal parent groups speaking out on behalf of their children, you have to wonder just how effective our messages to the community are.

A FUNDAMENTAL LEADERSHIP SKILL

Many leaders in the corporate world now understand that clear, two-way
communication is vital to the success of any organization and its leaders.
Jim Collins, in his best-selling book about making organizations better,
Good to Great, writes, "A primary task in taking a company [read: school
or school system] from good to great is to create a culture wherein people have a tremendous opportunity to be heard and, ultimately, for the
truth to be heard" (2001, p. 88).

"Communication is fundamental to building relationships and therefore to the ability to lead," says Jeswald W. Salacuse in his book *Leading
Leaders*. "Indeed, leadership could not exist without communication"
(2006, p. 23).

School leaders have been slower than their colleagues in industry to
take a long look at these issues. In the principal's, the assistant principal's, or the superintendent's office, we say, there is not a lot of time for
planning, and day-to-day issues tend to bleed out and fill available
hours. Maybe it's time to pause and look at the bigger picture. We are
educating students, not manufacturing and selling widgets, to be sure,
but we have much to learn from our business counterparts.

A BRIDGE, NOT A BUFFER

For the most part, institutions—including schools and school divisions—
have used public relations (and community relations and media relations and even employee relations) as a means of keeping people out.
Leaders send the press release or the employee newsletter with
management-filtered information and hope that it will keep the troops
happy. Communications becomes the buffer between leadership and
the stakeholders.

But it's just not working. The bond referendum is defeated; the school budget is cut; and the media continues to thrive on "bad news" stories.

There is a better way:

"Think of communication as a bridging activity," suggests scholar James Grunig (2006, p. 171), "an activity in which [a school or district] builds linkages with stakeholders . . . to transform and constitute the organization in new ways."

What if we used our communication to build bridges instead of moats? What if we came to understand what our parents really want and need in order to make our relationships work? What if we could create a reservoir of goodwill in the community that would carry us over the big bumps when we meet them? What if we could reduce the tensions within the faculties in our buildings and between faculties and other building employees? What if our students actually had a better climate in which to learn? Shouldn't we pay attention?

GOOD COMMUNICATION IS KEY TO COMMUNITY SUPPORT AND FUNDING

"One of the great ironies of school leadership today," says Nora Carr, a communication leader in schools and industry, "is that you can do a great job of educating students and communicating with parents, and still miss 78 to 80 percent of the people upon whose support public education—and your livelihood—depends.

"That's because the vast majority of people who pay taxes today in most communities small and large, do not have school-aged children. This means that we have to start paying more attention to school public relations and marketing, or pay the consequences" (Carr, 2005).

All school systems receive tax funding, but many communities must also pass public bonds and levies to fund operating budgets. Others use bond funding to support their system's capital improvement programs. Local schools supplement their operating budgets with donations, fundraisers, and business partnerships—all dependent on the goodwill of the citizens who often do not have school-aged children. These efforts, to be successful, must be fueled by good communication with parents and the community at large.

Carr calculates that "in most districts, if you spend $105,000 on better communications, you only need to recruit 15 new kindergartners at $7,000 each in per pupil funding to recoup your investment. If those 15 students stay in your district for 12 years, that initial investment in school marketing will yield more than $1 million."

That seems a relatively small investment for some potentially big returns—even in a small district with a modest budget.

COMMUNICATION IS CRUCIAL TO A LEADER'S JOB SECURITY

According to the American Association of School Administrators (AASA), the average tenure of a superintendent in 2007 is less than six years. The Council of Great City Schools reports the average tenure of an urban superintendent to be less than three years. Not very long.

Job security is an issue for principals too. Principals work close to the ground, where the action is. Parents care not so much about big policy issues, but more about what is happening in their child's school and, especially, in their child's classroom. So the credibility of a principal is key to parental satisfaction with school and the school system, and good communication makes a substantial contribution to that credibility.

No leader wants to fail. No superintendent or principal goes to the office in the morning looking to mess up. But—and this may surprise you—what causes a superintendent or principal to lose his or her job, more often than not, is *not* how she designed the new instructional initiative or how he managed the building renovation. Recent studies show that what brings the leader down is his or her inability to communicate with staff members and the community:

- In a California study, the major reason most principals were fired was poor interpersonal communications (Davis, 1998).
- In Tennessee, when superintendents ranked career-threatening skill deficiencies of principals, atop the list was a failure to work "cooperatively with faculty and staff" (Matthews, 2002).

- In yet another study, the mistakes by a principal most often identified by teachers were in human relations and interpersonal communications, specifically, a lack of trust and an uncaring attitude
  (Bulach, Boothe, and Pickett, 1998).
- The National School Public Relations Association conducted surveys and interviews of leading superintendent search firms to discover what qualities and skills were most important in the hiring of
  a new superintendent and which were lacking in those superintendents who were not successful in their positions. Along with
  leadership and *vision, communication skills* were ranked as the
  most desired by school boards in the hiring of a new superintendent. The *"lack of communication and the failure to keep people informed"* was the chief factor affecting the failure of a superintendent (Bagin, 2007b, p. 6).

School leaders are not alone. Research across many industries indi-
cates that leaders often fail because of "communicative incompetence"
(Kowalski, Peterson, and Fusarelli, 2007).

KIDS ARE THE CHIEF REASON WHY
COMMUNICATION MATTERS

Students learn better when adults communicate well. The need for good
communication in our schools is great because the needs of our students
are great. Students matter.

Good communication increases parent involvement in the school
(Henderson and Mapp, 2002). Many school and family collaborations
have demonstrated that parent involvement is a key ingredient in higher
student achievement (Cary, 2006, pp. 6–7). Good communication between the school and parents—and between the school district and the
community—creates a climate of trust and respect in which teachers
can teach and students can learn. Good communication builds a team—
that team we are always talking about—that team that surrounds and
supports a student so that he or she can succeed.

THE ENGINE OIL LIGHT IS BLINKING!

Four school stories appeared in the local paper one day last week:

- A large school system is facing a $2 million budget cut. In presenting his proposed budget to the school board, the superintendent outlined half the cuts and was quoted as saying that he "hoped" that the county government "will fill the rest of the shortage."
- In a nearby system, students protested loudly when a high school principal offered thirty dollars to any student who would name a perpetrator in a recent cafeteria food fight. "Bribery!" the students charged. District officials said that the practice of offering monetary rewards "happens a couple of times a year."
- In yet another large system in the area, a student was shot and killed in a drive-by shooting as she and a friend walked home from school. The principal labeled community claims that the shooting was gang-related as "hysteria."
- Back in the first system, a teacher and coach was charged with using his school computer to solicit sex with a minor. According to the school district spokesman, the teacher was placed on unpaid administrative leave, pending the outcome of the investigation. "We take very seriously the welfare of all the students in our schools," he said.

Ouch! In every one of these communities, the potential for rupture between school and community or between leadership and staff is huge. You have to hope that the lines of communication have been well tended and that the relationships among all the stakeholders are strong.

Every day in this country, we are designing and building new schools—smart schools, green schools, megaschools, community schools. In those buildings, we are constantly reframing how we work and how we teach and learn. We are differentiating curriculum; designing collaborative literacy, parallel curricula, and thinking strategies; and creating learning communities. We try to create and sustain excitement about what we are doing—both inside the building and out—by reorganizing the district management, by rebranding our programs, or by adding new and flashy technologies.

What we are *not* doing is focusing on the ways in which we are communicating with our stakeholders—our employees, our parents, our neighbors, the business owners, our elected officials, the taxpayers, or the reporters who write the stories. We are not paying enough attention to the relationships with those around us—the relationships that provide the long-term, sustained support for public education in our communities.

We send out newsletters. We have a website. We are front and center for back-to-school night. But many of the tools in our communication tool kits are outdated. We no longer understand our audiences. We speak in jargon. We take ourselves much too seriously and often convey to parents that we really don't care about their opinions.

A CALL FOR EXCELLENCE

Not just any communication attempt will get the job done. While much good communication is common sense, the first answer to a communication problem that surfaces is not always the best. It is too easy—especially with the help of a computer and color printer—to dash off a six-panel, four-color, two-fold brochure and consider the job is done. Did anyone ask to whom this brochure is addressed and what messages that audience really wants to hear? Did anyone ask who even reads brochures anymore? We make a lot of bad assumptions and waste a lot of time when we try to communicate without listening to our audiences first.

In today's world, only sustained communication efforts of the highest quality stand any real chance of making a difference. We don't have the luxury of saying, "Well, I already told the parents once." We know that that doesn't work. We also know that important messages must be communicated with attention to their emotional content. People pay far more attention to passion than they do to a list of facts.

We know too that each time we put communication on the back burner ("I'll get to that tomorrow") we risk further eroding our standing with parents and community. We risk our budgets, our test scores, and sometimes our jobs.

A NEW PARADIGM

High-quality communication does not occur accidentally. It happens when leaders are thoughtful and intentional about their efforts. It happens when leaders build strong personal relationships with their team and with their stakeholders. High quality communication is both carefully planned and the result of everyday interactions. It is a process—one that has no end. High quality communication rests on a mutual respect built between the school or school system and its various stakeholders. School leaders with good communication skills recognize and serve all the many and diverse audiences in a school community.

The superintendent whom we mentioned at the outset—the one with the customer-service bent—persisted in his initiative, despite the naysayers. He communicated clear standards for his employees. Wherever he went within the organization, the superintendent talked about the need for good communication and good service. He provided resources to increase service in places where it was most needed. He evaluated departments on their service. He found ways to reward individual staff members and departments for outstanding service. Within a year, there was a marked change in climate throughout the district.

In the pages that follow, we will look at some of the ways that school leaders can create that kind of effective communication and garner those kinds of successes in their own communities.

- We examine the assumptions that we make about the stakeholders with whom we communicate—assumptions that cause us to make big mistakes in our communication attempts.
- We offer a framework within which school leaders can look at the stakeholders they serve and gather information that will help them create strong, resilient relationships with those stakeholders.
- We propose plenty of practical suggestions for communicating in the difficult situations that principals and superintendents face every day.
- We tell stories of how school leaders have done it well. We look at some of our own bloopers. (The stories that we tell are real, though sometimes we have changed names and details to give cover to the innocent.)

We have worked with principals, assistant principals, and superintendents for a long time. We have spent most of our careers on the front lines. We have worked through difficult parent confrontations and combative meetings over such issues as education for gifted and talented children and special-needs children. We have helped principals lead their faculties in creating whole new school plans. We have worked with principals and public safety officials through hurricanes, drug busts, student slayings, faculty arrests, and a host of lock-down situations. We have worked through outbreaks of meningitis and tuberculosis, bomb threats, and even student counterfeit rings. (Young men spending lots of new twenty-dollar bills in the school cafeteria. What *were* they thinking?) And every time we said, "Well, now we've seen it all," there was a new challenge on our desks.

These experiences convinced us long ago that communication is a leadership issue. We believe that building good relationships—one by one—with all school stakeholders is the only way to create the effective and sustainable communication that is the foundation of a great school or school system.

The framework we have hammered out over time looks at leadership through a different lens. It's based on three assumptions:

- The key personal quality of effective leadership is integrity.
- The key skill of effective leaders is the ability to motivate cooperation from others.
- The key to motivating cooperation from others is high-quality communication in everyday interactions and small steps.

In these pages we share the wisdom that we have gained from working with the folks who make education happen for our young people—your colleagues. We believe that by building good relationships every day, a superintendent, school board members, a principal, or school staff members—indeed, any school leader—can create a better environment for teaching and learning and helping students thrive. That, for us, is the bottom line.

• • •

It is imperative that school leaders find motivation and resources to create long-range, comprehensive communication plans for their schools and districts. If they do not, they put their own careers, community support for their schools, and the opportunity to make their schools places where students thrive and learn in jeopardy.

I

THE RELATIONSHIPS

START WITH A WIN

Staying Ahead in a Changing World

When the rate of change is faster on the outside than the inside, the end is in sight.

—Jack Welsh

All you have to do is look out the window. We're trying to educate the community's children and, en route, we watch the wheels coming off the train. The rules of the game—the rules of the social interaction—keep changing.

We see signs of these changes every day in our own schools: Students carrying iPods and cell phones, parents asking to be at the table with staff when new bus routes are being created, elected officials putting test scores squarely in their sights. Because the changes are often subtle, we sometimes miss the larger, cumulative significance of what's happening. But at the end of the day, we feel a discomfort because things aren't going exactly as we'd planned. It's not like the old days.

We need to understand why the ante has been raised—and keeps on rising—and what we must do to lead effectively in these new times.

IT'S A NEW GAME

Technology has drastically changed the rules and tools of the communication game in the last ten years. In some school systems, as many as 90 percent of student homes are connected to the Internet, and parents and students are using the Web nonstop to find and share information. A growing number of homes of first generation Americans are connected, too, because the Internet provides an inexpensive link with friends and family members in their country of origin.

The nature of a school's audience has changed as well. In some school systems, English is no longer the language spoken in the majority of student homes. Indeed, it is not uncommon for a student body to include students who represent a hundred different languages. Communications in those schools must now go out in many translations to meet the needs of these children and their parents.

Boomer parents are being replaced by Generation X and even Millennial parents, whose wants and needs are very different. GenX parents use the Internet all the time. They want information easily accessible at whatever time they need it—even at two o'clock in the morning. They are looking for consistent, honest, up-front, friendly, personalized communication. The old ways of getting information out, that once satisfied boomer parents—the newsletter and monthly PTA meetings—no longer work.

OUR STAKEHOLDERS' EXPECTATIONS HAVE CHANGED

Not long ago, industry leaders like Nordstrom and the Ritz-Carlton set a new gold standard for world-class customer service. Corporations began training every employee in effective customer interaction. World-class customer service meant being sure that the customer walked away satisfied from every business transaction. As the notion spread, even the service at the corner drug store seemed to improve.

Then the bar got raised again. Customer *satisfaction* was no longer enough, the norm became customer *delight*. The practice of concierge services has reached down to all levels of the community. Today, if you are not *delighted* with your purchase, Zappos.com, the online shoe store giant, agrees to pay shipping charges *both* ways, *and* gives you a year to return the shoes you do not want. To meet its competition, USPS will now pick up packages at your door. Even the big box stores seek to enhance our shopping experience with greeters, liberal exchange policies, and personalized service. Is it any wonder that parents have no patience for an unanswered telephone in the school office?

Blink again. Now we are speeding past customer *delight* to *the full customer experience*. Like the Disney World experience: it's not about the rides, it's about making your dreams come true.

Want to design your own sneaker? (You will, if you are under twenty-one.) Go to the Converse Shoes website at www.converse.com, click on Custom Chucks (that stands for the Chuck Taylor model, if you're *over* twenty-one). At the site you can choose between high tops and low, select two colors for the outside of your new shoes, and separate colors for the laces, the lining, and the tongue. Then add a racing stripe and *your* logo on the heel. You can spend hours trying various combinations and watching the results appear on the screen. Assuming you have some time and design sense, what's not to like about that? It's not about the sneakers, it's about your ability to create your own unique world.

These experiences are designed to grab and hold your attention because you and your resources (money or support) will follow your attention. These experiences are designed to offer *total* delight and inspire customer loyalty of the highest order.

More and more, our young parents are asking for the same customer experience in school that they are being offered in other parts of their lives. They want this experience to be a part of their (and their child's) education. They aren't talking about gym class, they're talking about the Olympics.

The push for increased participation in the process comes at us from all sides: more staff committees and task forces, more PTA initiatives, extended teacher conferences, and direct e-mail contact with the principal and faculty. These demands sometimes leave us a bit confused and sometimes resentful. We thought we were here to educate the kids.

THE AIRWAVES ARE CROWDED—THE MESSAGES MIXED

There is another change that complicates the business of leadership. Each of us is bombarded with a staggering number of cues and messages every day from our families, workplaces, televisions, radios, iPods, and cell phones. Beyond these messages is the seduction of the Internet with its ever-growing resources. You can find just about *anything* online and stop to browse any number of other things on the way. These endless messages and opportunities clog our brain. It is hard for us to sort through all this information and understand what is reliable and useful. All this noise causes people to become leery of everything they hear. It makes them distrustful, even of the things we are trying to tell them about our schools.

Ironically, at the same time that the information glut is expanding, so is a demand to make life more personalized (like our sneakers). When we hear about events happening around the world, what we want to know is how that will affect us. Will *my* gas prices keep going up?

Today's parents find or create local blogs where they get the scoop on their own neighborhood. Occasionally, they get fired up about a districtwide school issue, but, mostly, they care about what happens in their own child's classroom. Just like my Chuck Taylors, they say, "I want my child's education to be designed just for her. No cookie-cutter solutions, please."

LEADERSHIP IN THIS CHANGING WORLD

The face of leadership is changing too. Businesses and corporations are struggling to find effective ways to lead in this new world. You only have to read the titles on the business shelves of any bookstore to understand how widespread the search is:

> *Leadership 101: What Every Leader Needs to Know,*
> *The 21 Indispensable Qualities of a Leader: Becoming the Person Others Will Want to Follow,*
> *The Leadership Challenge,*
> *The Leadership Pipeline: How to Build the Leadership Powered Company,* and even,
> *The Leadership Secrets of Santa Claus.*

To meet the challenges of this changing world, leaders in schools must also sharpen old tools and craft new ones. They must look at their day and their job through new lenses. Leaders need new models.

"The key to creating and sustaining [the successful twenty-first-century organization] is leadership—not only at the top of the hierarchy, with a capital *L*, but also in the more modest sense (*l*) throughout the enterprise. This means that over the next few decades we will see . . . a new form of organization emerge to cope with fast-moving and more competitive environments," says John Kotter, author and professor emeritus of Harvard Business School. And, he concludes, "As an observer of life in organizations, I think I can say with some authority that people who are making an effort to embrace the future are a happier lot than those who are clinging to the past" (Kotter, 1996, pp. 175, 186).

Here are five leadership models that are proving to be successful in this new environment that Kotter describes:

The Leader as Coach

We can all benefit from coaching or what Peter Senge and colleagues (1999, p. 106) describe as "experienced, compassionate guidance from people who have 'been there,' and who know how to manage and design the journey." (p. 106)

But, warns researcher and best-selling author Daniel Goleman and his colleagues (2002, p. 61), leaders who are focused exclusively on high performance "often think they're coaching when actually they're micromanaging or simply telling people how to do their jobs."

"The best coaches," Goleman says, "show a genuine personal interest in those they guide, and have an empathy for and an understanding of their employees" (1998, p. 147). Good coaches "acknowledge and reward people's strengths and accomplishments," "offer useful feedback," and "identify people's needs for further growth."

There are many reasons to develop our coaching skills. In schools, leaders are not only developing employees, they are developing parents and volunteers as well. Working with the volunteer chairperson of a parent committee or even with a school board member often requires coaching skills.

"Strong coaching or mentoring helps employees perform better, enhances loyalty and job satisfaction, leads to promotions and pay increases, and lowers rates of turnover" (Goleman, 1998, p. 147). Among parents, strong coaching develops a corps of loyal school supporters.

Coaching takes time but offers rich dividends. It provides the opportunity for that personal face-to-face contact that increases in importance as our use of technology increases.

The Leader as Caring Listener

"People will forget what you say. People will forget what you do. But people will never forget how you make them feel," says psychologist and trainer, Dr. Joseph Mancusi.

In a time when everyone is *sending* messages, listening has become a lost art. Careful listening is a way to make people feel cared about. In this world where we are bombarded with so many impersonal messages, more than anything else, people want to be listened to. Even if you don't solve their problem, listening will make them feel better. Listening is the beginning of all relationships.

When you pay attention, your world gets bigger. When you listen thoughtfully, you let go of your own expectations and prejudices. People sense that you are open to their ideas and feelings. They feel safe and are more willing to reach out to you. Listening slows down the conversation and allows solutions to thorny problems to rise to the surface (Garmston and Wellman, 1999).

> The people I have met who are most effective at changing the world have two qualities. On the one hand, they are extraordinarily committed, body and soul, to the change they want to see in the world, to a goal larger than themselves. On the other hand, they are extraordinarily open to listen to what is happening in the world, in others, and in themselves.
>
> —Adam Kahane

Listening is also a problem-solving tool with bottom-line implications. Industry research has demonstrated that, each year, businesses spend an average of 30 percent of their income to fix mistakes. Schools and school districts are probably not much different. Many mistakes are made because we don't listen carefully in the beginning. We make assumptions about our clients and their wants and needs. If we listen better, we will spend fewer dollars mopping up.

> *Creative Listening*
> * *Take turns talking and listening*
> * *Pause before speaking*
> * *Repeat what you thought you heard*
> * *Convey your attention with your body language*
> * *Eliminate distractions*
> * *Focus on the message, not the messenger*
> * *Listen without feeling you need to act*
> * *Honor the speaker's views*
>
> —Robert Garmston

The Leader as Truth Teller

Nothing destroys relationships faster than the suspicion of deception. We have to look no further than the front page of our newspapers every day to confirm that.

"We know when we're being spun," one parent says of her school's leadership. "We resent it."

Telling the truth is particularly important when the news is bad. At the end of the second year of No Child Left Behind implementation, a local school "did not meet standards" for a second time and was immediately labeled "failing" by the local press. The principal crafted letters to the parents and planned community meetings to present and explain the school's test numbers, describe the measures that the school would take to remedy the difficulties, and offer parents the transfer option required by law.

Because of her careful work, only a few parents chose to transfer their children to other schools the following year. Instead, the principal received thanks from the parents for her forthright approach.

In the media, a bad news story told quickly and completely is a one-day story. A bad news story that leaks or that is badly told at the outset can stretch on for days or even weeks. Get out front and tell the truth. If the news is bad enough, tell it yourself. Answer the tough questions immediately. Don't hide. Honesty is the bedrock of strong relationships.

The Leader as Risk Taker

"You might as well fall flat on your face as lean over too far backwards," said James Thurber.

With our world around us changing as quickly as it is, we cannot possibly know with any certainty whether the steps we take today, or the programs we put in place for our students, will turn out in five years to be the best ones. We take calculated risks every day.

To take risks with confidence, a savvy observer told us, a school leader needs to be comfortable in his or her own skin. It is risky to invite reporters to wander the halls. It is risky to put parent committees in charge of events. It is risky to entrust leadership roles to staff members. But the principal or superintendent "comfortable in his or her skin" will reap the rewards of sharing information and responsibility.

A middle school principal complained that her faculty meetings were so dull that even she was bored. So she took a risk. Instead of talking to the teachers for an hour every month, she used the time to divide the staff into teams, giving each team a real and thorny administrative issue to tackle.

"The teachers worked really hard," she reported several months later with some surprise. "They came up with great solutions!"

Risky though it may seem, keep your doors open. Not just your office door, but your classroom doors as well.

In one neighborhood elementary school we know, the principal always welcomed parents into her office. "She loved to talk with us," the parent of a third grader told us. "But, in the four years my son has been in that school, I have been allowed in his classroom exactly once! Parents are forbidden. There are no room mothers for the classrooms, no parent chaperones for field trips. How do you think that makes us feel?"

A University of California economist, David Romer, had a hunch about risk taking. He speculated that though people have goals in life and say that they will do everything possible to attain those goals, in fact, their behavior does not always follow.

Romer did a study of football teams facing fourth-down situations. From his numbers, he concluded that, to be successful, teams must regularly press forward on fourth down, rather than attempting a field goal or punting—even when the score is tied and even when the team is playing in their own territory. *On average, he concluded, teams do not take the risks they need to take to win the game* (Vedantam, 2007, italics added).

His study raises some interesting questions for leaders. We say we are ready to push forward, but what happens on fourth down? Are we taking the risks we need to succeed?

The Leader as Storyteller

What better way for a leader to lead (and teach) than to tell stories? We all love stories. We read fairy tales to our children. We tell each other stories about our lives. We read biographies of heroes and villains. These stories teach us, even while they are entertaining us. Aesop got it.

Vivid stories and pictures capture our imagination. It was no accident that, in a desperate battle for hearts and minds, the Bush administration refused to release pictures of the flag-draped coffins of U.S. servicemen returning to Dover Air Force Base. At the same time that the *Washington Post* daily printed a story, with picture, of a funeral of a war casualty at Arlington Cemetery. We remember stories. Stories can move us to action.

Especially in an unsteady and changing world, stories reassure people. Stories speak to our emotions and add passion to our determination. Without that passion, your mission will stall. Stories give people the courage to get through hard times—if those stories make people believe they will prevail. (Remember Winston Churchill and FDR?)

Stories give hope. Remember, in schools we are practicing education, but we are also selling dreams: Jenny can become an engineer, Johnny can go to Africa to work with AIDS patients, Eleanor can become a high-powered lawyer, and Elliott can become the world's best chef. The dreams of our students are some of our most important stories.

We can honor the stories of our graduates who have returned to work in our community. We can remember together how our school division and community struggled to establish our students' equal rights and celebrate the gains we have made. As leaders, we can paint pictures of how much we can accomplish if we work together on our shared goals.

By far, the most popular publication we ever produced was a small six-panel, accordion-fold brochure, featuring the ten teachers who had been selected to receive the local Chamber of Commerce excellence awards that year. Instead of listing all the benefits of public education, each panel had the picture of a teacher and quotes from students about his or her teaching. Each personal testimony spoke to the finest qualities of teaching. Each panel had a story to tell.

"It is through language that we create the world, because it's nothing until we describe it. And when we describe it, we create distinctions that govern our actions. *To put it another way, we do not describe the world we see, but we see the world we describe*" (Jaworski, 1996, p. 178).

If we tell our stories well enough, we make our stakeholders see and value the work that happens in schools.

The Leader as Relationship Builder

The most important skill we must cultivate as leaders is our skill as builder of relationships.

"Wealth in a knowledge economy comes from connections," says futurist David Zach. The wealth of our schools depends on our ability to make connections within the educational system and beyond—connections that bring resources to bear on the important work taking place in the classroom. The strength of those connections is the test of our leadership.

In the long run, the relationships that school leaders build with staff members, students, parents, and community are more important to the success of the school than any individual program. School leaders who know how to get things done—you know them—have a wide network of sturdy relationships throughout the organization and beyond.

A seasoned principal arrived at his new high school with all the innocence and promise that goes with a new job. Two years before, the school board, wanting to move the district's teaching and learning quickly online, had decided to issue a laptop to every high school teacher and student. One of the complaints that awaited the new principal was that the teachers were not using the laptops in the classroom and that the students were only using them for their e-mail and Facebook adventures. Indeed, criticism of the laptop distribution program had already made it into the pages of the local weekly.

The principal moved quickly. He identified a small number of key teachers from various departments who together taught a large number of students every week. He invited these teachers to meet with him regularly to explore ways to use the laptops in their teaching. Word of the new workgroup quickly spread in the building. Other teachers asked to join the group, but at first the principal chose to keep the original group intact.

It soon became clear to everyone in the building that the principal had built a special relationship with these teachers and that computer use in the classroom was being rewarded. Other teachers began borrowing and using the new techniques. Training gradually was extended to other teachers who stepped forward. By the end of the school year, laptop use by both faculty and students had risen sharply. In place of the barbs, the principal had built strong relationships with his staff.

Schools can also no longer afford to isolate themselves on their own instructional islands. A superintendent who agrees to sit on the governing board of the chamber of commerce or a principal who is a trustee of the local community foundation builds important ties between the community and the schools. Working with the symphony on a state arts grant for student concerts, cooperating with the local medical school to bring services to students from low-income homes, inviting industry leaders into meaningful supporting advisory roles in the district—these are all part of a successful day's work.

MAKING THE CONNECTIONS

So what does this have to do with communication and how does this get me to a win?

In Chinese, the written character for "crisis" also means "opportunity." These uncertain times offer us some stunning opportunities to win support for our schools. Because the world is changing so fast on the outside, parents and community members look to schools as the glue that will hold things together and the place where things will get fixed. Watch how often the community uses the school system as the playing field on which to work out its anxieties.

- Terrorist attack? Are the *schools* prepared?
- Chemical spill? Do the *schools* have enough water stored for shelter-in-place?
- Epidemic? What will the *schools* do to prevent its spread?

As the temperature outside rises, the line between community issues and school concerns get blurred.

Issues like these give schools opportunities to show their stuff. Leaders who listen to their stakeholders and respond thoughtfully, leaders who tell the truth and take risks to meet their stakeholders' needs, leaders who build relationships and are able to engage their parents and students and community in a common effort—these leaders create a sturdy network of support for their schools and districts. These are the leaders who, in the midst of chaos, can sustain an environment that allows teaching and learning to happen.

The leadership skills that help build a sound community in a changing world are the same skills that help a leader move that community forward and transform itself in response to the new world. Strong relationships make change possible. Leaders who embark on big initiatives without those relationships solidly in place are headed for trouble.

These skills are, in fact, all communication skills. Communication—which has all too often been an afterthought—takes center stage in an uncertain, changing world. Sharpen your communication skills and you position yourself for success.

• • •

Faced with the challenges of a changing world, school leaders must learn to use their communication skills to help shape the future. Skillful superintendents and principals have the opportunity to lead change and effectively meet the demands of the new world outside. To do that successfully, leaders need to be relationship builders, careful listeners, truth tellers, risk takers, and storytellers.

For reflection

1. In what ways are you best at building relationships with stakeholders?
2. How many times today did you catch yourself listening carefully?
3. What risky situations do you and your school/district face this year?
4. When are you most tempted to hide or gloss over the truth?
5. What stories does your school/district have to tell?

BUILD TRUST

Demonstrating Respect, Competence, and Integrity

You can't win on defense.

—Anonymous

Did you ever think you would stand in a line for a four-dollar cup of coffee, order it with strange terms (venti or grande?) and wait in yet a second line for your caramel macchiato? Starbucks changed our expectations for drinking coffee. They did it by nurturing public trust. Because we trust that we are in for a treat, we suspend our belief that the coffee's too expensive or too much trouble.

Why do we trust them? It's all for the promise of what Starbucks has to offer: they make a darned good cup of coffee (they're competent), they support the community through good works (they've got integrity), and they welcome us with cushy chairs (they respect us). Take off your shoes and sit awhile.

Seeking to build trusting relationships with parents, staff, and communities, school leaders can learn a lot from Starbucks and other businesses like them. Starbucks knows that high trust brings enormous benefits and the lack of trust comes with big costs. Their success comes from engaging the community in its vision of coffee drinking. We have a vision too, and we should be engaging our communities.

UNCONDITIONAL TRUST: IT'S NOT HAPPENING

Yesterday's school leaders didn't have to think about building trust, they simply had it. They selected textbooks, ordered new playground equipment, and administered discipline, all with little input from outside the school walls. There was neither a need nor a call for it. Schools had unconditional trust from a community who accepted their decisions. Like churches and hospitals, public schools were regarded as venerable institutions and thus beyond reproach.

Today, leaders operate in a much different environment. Headlines shout education's worst cases, politicians pile on, and urban legends abound. The public is understandably wary and requires reassuring. The successful school leader steps into the trust void and fills it with communication practices that rebuild the trust.

THE TRUST ELEPHANT

Steven M. R. Covey believes that trust has two components: character and competence (2006). "Simply put, trust means confidence. The opposite of trust—distrust—is suspicion. When you trust people, you have confidence in them—in their integrity and in their abilities. When you distrust people, you are suspicious of them—of their integrity, their agenda, their capabilities, or their track record" (p. 5).

Once trust is established—genuine character and competence-based trust—almost everything else falls into place, Covey (2006) says. Trust allows us to operate with greater speed, lower cost, and improved results. Without trust, the cost is significant.

Trust is the elephant in the room when we're trying to determine why bad things happen to good leaders. We need only to look at newspaper headlines to see examples of schools (and other institutions, for that matter) paying what Covey calls a "trust tax." Leaders pay the tax in the form of diverted attention, added stress, wasted time, and lost money. Without trust, small incidents spiral out of control and become all consuming. While each occurrence has different players and details, the origin of the escalation is almost always the same: lack of trust.

For example, a high school principal we know spent over two months mopping up after he suspended a popular athlete for a violation of school rules. A seemingly routine decision turned into a flashpoint on which the community rallied against the principal, hired an attorney, and challenged the school's competence and integrity. At the heart of the matter: lack of trust between the community and the school. Here's how that issue played out:

- The principal refused to meet in person with the athlete's parents following the suspension.
- School leadership ignored earlier charges of selective enforcement of school rules.
- School staff was divided in its support of the principal.

Each of these issues might have been addressed differently with responses that demonstrated respect, competence, and integrity. What if the principal had shown personal regard for the parents by meeting and listening? What if leadership had taken action by creating a task force to address charges of selective enforcement? What if the principal had worked to build a culture of trust with the entire school staff? While the principal's suspension decision held in this case, the further loss of trust between school and community made this a hollow victory.

Trust and Schools
- Principals, staff and parents are interdependent.
- Trust is a product of everyday interactions.
- Parents use four benchmarks to discern the intentions of those in schools:
  - Respect
  - Personal regard for others
  - Competence
  - Integrity

(Kochanek, 2005)

COMMUNICATING RESPECT

Ever had any of the following experiences?

- The phone call (at home!) from the doctor (personally!) who asks about your recovery the day after a minor surgery.
- The rental car service person who continues to refer to you by name after pulling up your reservation. (May we upgrade you to a convertible, Mrs. Littlefield?)
- The air conditioning repair person who accommodates your schedule by showing up before normal working hours.

Practices like these communicate respect. They make us feel safe and in competent hands. Consistent messages of respect and the repetition of sound practices create the strong bonds that hold together a trusting relationship.

Harvard professor and author Edward M. Hallowell, MD (1999), writes about the value of the trust connection, which he defines as the human moment that can occur anytime two or more people are together, paying attention to one another. It takes a skilled leader, Hallowell writes, to create an atmosphere of positive connection. Usually what makes the biggest difference, he says, is respect for the individual person.

We first discern respect through simple, everyday exchanges. In the hurly-burly of everyday school life, the niceties are easy to overlook. The successful leader plans the details that translate into trust. She is careful to avoid common missteps that can destroy relationships:

- A parent calls the school's main number during the day and the call goes into voice mail.
- A teacher is hurried out of the principal's office before his complaint can be fully aired.
- A receptionist shows her annoyance at a parent's question.

Slights like these undermine respect. When it happens to any of us, we file the experience away only to resurrect it when it's time to decide whether we're willing to extend our trust on more serious issues. Parents do the same.

On the other hand, messages of trust can also be communicated in small, deliberate ways. Your message may be sent in the form of smiling faces, visitor parking signs, returned phone calls, and acknowledgment of concerns. It's a climate that tells stakeholders that they matter. They're safe with you. You'll treat them right.

A leader builds respect by seeking out occasions to have conversations with folks:

- Talking with a small group of parents over punch in the cafeteria. ("Thanks for coming out to the meeting tonight. How'd you think it went?")
- Arriving early for and/or staying after meetings. (We all know that's when the "real" work is accomplished.)
- Stopping by a teacher's classroom before school just to chat. ("How you feeling today, Ms. Moynehan?" Prepare yourself: What questions will you ask? What will you do with the answers?)

One of the greatest compliments we've heard given to an administrator is "he really listened to what we had to say." Translated: he respected me. High praise indeed.

ANTICIPATING STAKEHOLDER NEEDS

People come to the school with a variety of anxieties. Will I fit in? Will I know what to do? Will my child be treated as an individual? Will I know how to help? You bump respect up a notch by anticipating these kinds of stakeholder needs. Some examples of communication practices that ease feelings of vulnerability include:

- A PTA meeting with translators.
- A school newsletter that allows parents to skim for information.
- A front office that has preprinted directions to hand parents who ask how to get to a common destination.
- A message returned sooner than expected.
- A personal response from the principal.
- A knack for remembering people's names.

Tending to small details that make a big difference will ease stake-holder's anxieties, demonstrate your respect and pave the way to a trust-ing relationship.

What We Have Here Is a Failure to Communicate Trust

An assistant principal (AP) told us recently how frustrated he was with his boss. Even though she was on vacation—the Caribbean, mind you— the principal continued to monitor and responded to e-mail. This vigi-lance, she believed, communicated caring, dedication, and commitment. The AP saw it quite differently.

Her pool-side missives symbolized to him a lack of trust in his ability to be in charge. Her involvement in day-to-day decisions, including whether to order blue or a green pens for an event's give-away, nearly pushed him over the edge.

"Did she really think that she was the only one who could make that kind of decision?" he asked, describing what he believed was a vote of no confidence. On her return, he raised the issue in a conversation that led both to an understanding of how powerful communication is in sending messages of trust—and distrust.

WHY PARENTS TRUST (AND DISTRUST) TEACHERS

Teachers, too, benefit from engaging in intentional practices to commu-nicate respect. One parent describes her son's "extremely competent first-grade teacher." She said she drew that conclusion from the respect the teacher showed for her son during the parent-teacher conference.

Celeste, the parent, was worried that her quiet son would be lost in the classroom if a teacher "wrote him off" as withdrawn. How pleased she was, then, in the parent-teacher conference when the teacher used "reserved" to describe the boy, rather than "shy" or "introverted." A sub-tle difference in word choice, one that shows respect for the child, made a big difference to Celeste. It gave her the confidence, the trust, she was seeking. Nuanced language is a powerful tool that can signal respect.

Sue, a parent of a special-needs child, had a broken trust relationship with her daughter Anna's teacher. Sue would see the teacher when she came to pick up Anna after school, yet the teacher rarely made eye con-tact, engaged her in any conversation, called her by name, or gave her any informal reports on Anna's progress. It took several days before the teacher returned a phone call from Sue, and then gave no apology or reason for the delay. Sue said it was impossible for her to trust the school without the basic respect from the teacher she felt entitled to, and she asked that Anna be switched to another teacher.

COMMUNICATING COMPETENCE

A while ago we were booked on a flight from Montreal to Washington that ended up being cancelled because of weather. An airline official calmed a frustrated crowd of 100 travelers with concrete explanations. The official gave us facts we could understand: the temperature, the wind speed, the amount of snow. He explained clearly the danger of flying in these conditions. Then, he delineated what the airline company was doing for us—transportation to a nearby hotel, dinner, and breakfast the next morning.

Airline officials did many other things, including being sympathetic, delivering frequent updates, and answering questions. They were clearly in charge of the situation. They were respectful and competent. We trusted them. Yes, there were a few wildly disgruntled passengers. (You know who we mean.) But the great majority of us were satisfied fliers who believed we were in good hands.

When the stakes of a situation get raised, when a leader holds the fate of others in his or her hands, it's necessary to communicate both respect *and* competence. Being successful often means keeping people calm and confident that you have the ability to take care of their needs. High stakes situations that schools face include disciplinary hearings, IEP conferences, and selections for induction into the National Honor Society. Each of these situations can be effectively managed with the communication of competence—especially when a solid foundation of respect is in place.

Leaders communicate competence by delivering concrete messages. The messages from the airline company were simple, uncluttered, and clear. They were delivered with authority and addressed the passengers' needs. Officials were patient, open, and clearly in charge. They offered workable options and had solutions to most of our problems. All of these qualities communicate competence.

COMMUNICATING INTEGRITY

While competence is most often communicated through language, integrity is discerned through *alignment of your words and actions*. Developing a focused message to articulate who you are and what you're all about—your vision—is an important first step.

Dr. Robert Spillane (former superintendent of Fairfax County Public Schools) was well known across the large school division for his focused message. His mantra, "Keep the main thing the main thing," reminded stakeholders that all their actions must be rooted in what is best for children. Dr. Spillane never missed an opportunity to bring a conversation back to the main thing.

Building a culture of integrity involves more than message and intention. Behavior counts. George Allen's second campaign for the United States Senate in 2006 is a case in point. The Virginia politician's offhand remark at a political rally cost him reelection. Referring to a college student working for the senator's opponent, Allen pointed in the crowd to the young man, who was filming the event, and referred to him as "maccaca."

Caught on tape, the gaffe moved to the top of the news and traveled across the world on the Internet. When Allen gave the requisite apology days later, he added that he didn't know the term "maccaca" was derisive and he did not intend to insult. He claimed his intentions were honest. The public didn't buy his explanation, the story continued to play, and Allen's attempts to mitigate didn't help.

His integrity, a key to engendering trust, was being questioned. Allen's strategy to save his character, and thus the election, was to persuade voters to shift their focus from his words to his heart. It did not fly. His behavior was what the public read. Allen's trust account was overdrawn.

Even a statement by the candidate's mother attesting to her son's good heart did no good. A debate, fueled by the question of racism, was the headline for days and played prominently in the campaign that Allen eventually lost. Intentions don't cut it in a 24/7 news world.

Some leaders are naturals. They seem to know intuitively how to build the relationships that engender trust. They just follow their nose. The rest of us, though, need to practice—we need to be intentional about communicating respect, demonstrating competence, and acting with integrity. It's all about building trust.

• • •

- DO create everyday communications that build trust. Be trustworthy.
- DON'T believe that telling people they can trust you will have any impact on their beliefs. Think Shakespeare—"Methinks he doth protest too much."
- DO know that parents judge school competence in large part through successful connections with their child's teacher.
- DO know that bureaucratic practices are a barrier to trust. When was the last time you accepted "it's our policy" as a final answer?

For reflection

1. How has your school community's reputation been impacted by trust, or the lack of trust?
2. Consider a low-stakes interaction you recently encountered. What behaviors in you or others demonstrated respect or personal regard?
3. Consider a high-stakes interaction you recently encountered. What behaviors in you or others demonstrated competence or integrity?

(3)

WIN BY PERSUASION

Using Communication to Gain Friends and Influence People

The single biggest problem in communication is the illusion that it has taken place.

—George Bernard Shaw

In August 2006, Ned Lamont won a stunning victory in the Connecticut Democratic Primary over longtime incumbent Senator Joe Lieberman. Lamont started his race with no name recognition and no organization, but he had a clear vision and some resources (in this case, both talent and money) to get the job done. Whether or not you support his views, you have to admire his skill.

There is much that a principal or superintendent can learn from candidate Lamont. Ned Lamont ran his campaign at the grassroots. He was on the street talking about his ideas. He met with citizens in their homes, drank their coffee, and listened to their concerns. For months.

At the same time, he and his managers used the Web consistently and effectively to move the campaign forward. His team gathered as many names of likely voters and volunteers as they could find. They put their lists on computer. Using those lists, they regularly contacted folks all across the state and asked for their votes. His campaign used one of the oldest tools of persuasion and one of the newest, together, to get the job done.

To be sure, Lamont campaigned on a major issue that was already gaining momentum. To be sure, his opponent made mistakes. But Lamont stayed close to the ground. He kept his messages simple, clear, and consistent. And he was available. He built relationships that people felt they could trust.

HOW LEADERS PERSUADE

Superintendents and principals have a lot of persuading to do. Sometimes the job is a big one—like selling a new bell schedule, and sometimes it is just introducing the new third-grade teacher. The concerned audience isn't always parents. Sometimes, it's the whole staff, or the teachers, or the city council. Sometimes it's the neighbors. (Ever tried to move three new trailers on-site or cut down trees at the back property line?) Leading the way into new territory almost always means there is a lot of persuading to do.

That's why the Lamont campaign is so instructive. Many principals we know already use the strategies he used so successfully. A young and energetic principal, Sharon, took the reigns of a middle school following the long tenure of an established principal. This was a school that might have been primed to resist change. Almost immediately, Sharon began meeting with small groups of the faculty, moving systematically through the departments (the Ned Lamont neighborhood meetings in another guise). She set out to establish strong lines of communication with her teachers, listening carefully to their opinions, and responding quickly—where she could—to their requests. She asked her administrative team to identify the trouble spots in the school and went to work on the hard issues immediately.

When we met up with her only a few months into her tenure, the building was humming happily. She ran an anonymous survey of her faculty and discovered that already she had gained the trust of many. They liked her small-group approach (as labor-intensive as it was for her) and felt that they were gaining a voice in the school.

Sharon's leadership style was transparent—everyone knew where she was headed. Her communication with staff members was clearly two-way. The survey and the small groups helped her to identify what she called the "elephants still in the room," and she had gone to work immediately to address those thorny issues. Sharon turned a potentially difficult situation into an opportunity to establish herself in her new community.

Sometime later, we met Linda—a superintendent in a small district for many years—who had already begun to lead her staff toward more effective use of the Web for their internal communications. Linda was sending all her memos, alerts, and commendations electronically and was delighted that her staff had followed her lead. But, now, she found everyone was complaining about how full their e-mail boxes were with top-down mail. "How," she asked, "can we streamline what comes from my office so that everyone will value—and read—what we send?"

Linda recognized that, having converted her staff to e-mail and Web, she had a new challenge before her: how to stay relevant and readable. She took action. For a month, she printed every piece of e-mail she sent out and collected it in a notebook. She asked employees in her office to review each e-mail and make suggestions about its urgency, its target audiences, and whether this was the most appropriate way to deliver that particular message.

Based on what she heard, the superintendent revised how she and her leadership staff used e-mail and the Web internally. They cut down on the traffic. Only the most important and urgent messages came directly from the superintendent by e-mail. Other items were posted on a Web "bulletin board" that staff members could access and read at their leisure. This helped everyone be clear about the relative importance of news items and determine when there was a need for quick response. The new system drew rave reviews.

Sharon used face time with her staff—and Linda captured the capabilities of technology—to reach out to employees, providing information and the opportunity for response.

TRANSPARENCY COUNTS

"Openness empowers people," say James Carville and Paul Begala (2002, p. 97). "As a leader, including the people you work with in the information loop empowers them" (p. 97).

"Successful campaigns," they continue, "place a premium on creativity, initiative and action. But people can't think for themselves if they don't have the information on which to base a decision. You can't delegate authority and then hoard information" (p. 98). Carville and Begala worked on political campaigns, but the campaign could just as easily be a campaign to bring neighborhood support back to the school after years of bad test scores or a campaign to reassure parents after a series of bullying incidents in the building. We have never met a superintendent or a principal who lost by opening up an issue, carefully and thoughtfully, with his or her community.

Time consuming? You bet. A challenging leadership mode to sustain over time? Absolutely. But the most successful leaders we know—and the ones in industry that we read about—all manage to stay available and keep communications open, even in the toughest of times.

"It takes an enormous amount of creativity, energy and leadership to bring someone along with you who perhaps doesn't get it at first," Carville and Begala agree. But if you are lucky and keep at it, eventually you will transform him "out of his foolhardiness" (p. 37).

No coach wins a game by what he or she knows. You win by what your players have learned.

—Coach Al McGuire, Marquette University,
1977 national basketball champions

USE THE TECHNOLOGY

Used well, new technologies can support your efforts. Many school systems now employ Web and e-mail—even blogging—to reach their parents, staff members, and community members quickly and easily. A number of effective telephone dial-out and automated e-mail systems—scaled for either a single school or a whole school division—are now on the market. Some schools employ both phone and e-mail to be sure that they reach not only tech-savvy families, but households not yet connected to the Internet. Telephone dial-out systems also make it easier to reach families in more than one language.

It seems curious—though certainly helpful—that these mechanical systems can actually seem personal to the user. Parents are often comforted by hearing the principal's recorded voice. Even e-mails can be made to seem intimate.

Some years ago, when the school division that we were working for set up a push e-mail system (the ability to segment audiences and electronically send messages, for instance, to all parents in a school, or just those in the third grade, or to all English teachers) the Web maestra in the communications department suggested that each message from the superintendent begin "Dear [first name of the recipient]." Kitty was horrified.

"I don't want to get a message 'Dear Kitty' from someone I've never met! That's ridiculous!" she exclaimed.

Well, persuaded by expert advice, we tried it anyway, and sure enough the superintendent began getting e-mail back:

"Thank you so much for the information. It was very helpful. *And thank you for making the message seem so personal.*"

"I so appreciated your sending the message to me *personally*. Thanks. Please send me more."

And on, and on. Wow, were we wrong!

Grassroots 101

A principal received an electronic request for information from an anxious parent new to the school. The principal was ready, having already created a number of boilerplate responses that she could quickly customize. She responded immediately. She addressed the parent's hopes and fears. She referred to the child by name and invited the parent for coffee. Here's how the parent responded: "From your e-mail alone I know that my son will be attending a great school." Preparation and attention to detail—critical elements for effective grassroots persuasion.

Whether by computer or recorded phone tape, a special message from the principal or superintendent concerning important events carries weight with employees and in the community—provided the messages are not overlong and the medium is not overused. Nothing riles a parent faster than a phone mail or e-mail box overflowing with messages about every PTA fund-raiser and booster event.

"I am *so* sorry I ever gave them my e-mail address," one dad told us recently. "I need to hear how my son is doing in class, but I *don't* need to hear how the gift wrap sales are progressing."

This is the same issue that superintendent Linda had with her staff members. Helping your audience discriminate between what is really important and what is only temporarily important is key. And note also that the dad is talking about what is important to *him* as a parent—not to the PTA president, who may well be very concerned about gift wrap sales.

The question to ask always before sending a message is "what does *my client* want to know about this matter?" (If he doesn't want to know what you think he should know, then you have a different job to do.)

BALANCE IS THE KEY

Management guru Jim Collins (2001) wrote a book about what it takes to make good companies into great companies. In his chapter on technology, Collins says "the good-to-great companies [that he studied] used technology as an accelerator of momentum, not a creator of it" (p. 162). Technology itself will not design or bring about change, but careful use of technology to support your work will help you achieve your goals. So, you have set up your living room chats. You also have your computers fired up and ready to go. The other skill you need in your personal persuasion toolbox is the ability to balance up-front, open contact with your people and the creative use of the technology—knowing when to send a blast e-mail to everyone in the school and when to sit down in small groups and talk about the issue. That balance was the Ned Lamont secret.

The balance is different in every community. It can shift with the issues. Parents and staff members will probably be a whole lot less sensitive about a fifteen-minute shift in summer office hours than they will be about moving to block scheduling. The balance can also shift as affected audiences change. Finding the right balance each time is a mark of your leadership.

How easy it is to assure ourselves that if people don't understand the wisdom of our decisions, it is really *their* problem. We once worked for a superintendent who regularly made that mistake. He was a bright man, quick to assess problems and see solutions. He was all about kids. But he was also quick to assume that issues that were clear to him would be clear for everyone. Once he figured out what needed to be done, he was in a hurry to do the right thing. He never stopped to explain. He never met with staff or parents to be sure that they were with him. In the end, he lost his constituency and his job.

Candidate Lamont stayed on the front lines. To persuade the people to vote for him, he met them where they were living and working—on the streets and in their homes. He recognized the value of human contact in the very impersonal world in which we find ourselves. He answered questions. He listened. *And* he used the new technologies to support his effort. School leaders today should do no less.

(Postscript: Candidate Lamont did not win the general election— sometimes in life you don't win—but his primary race stands as a model for changing people's minds.)

• • •

Persuasion is one of a leader's most powerful communication tools. Used carefully, both personal, face-to-face communication and the Web and e-mail can be effective tools for school leaders as they work to bring about a change of attitudes in their constituents.

For reflection

1. Considering the limits on your time, what are the key issues on the table on which you need to be most persuasive?
2. In what types of face-to-face contacts are you most successful? (One-on-one? Groups?)
3. How is the organization currently using technology for "personal" contact with your stakeholders?
4. What technologies could you be using to provide better communication?

LISTEN TO THE NEW GENERATIONS

Reaching Out to Those Who Expect to Connect

> New leaders must invent the future while dealing with the past.
>
> — Margaret Wheatley

Thirty-year-old Cassie Jenkins began the school selection process for her son before he was born.

By her sixth month of pregnancy, Jenkins was searching the Internet, talking to neighbors, and reading local newspapers with a new sense of purpose: finding the best school. Sending him to Park Street Elementary, a public school just across the street, did not seem to Jenkins to be a foregone conclusion.

Jenkins's actions are trademark Generation X, the moniker given those born between 1964 and 1987 (Howe and Strauss, 2007), who are parents of many of the children in our schools today. Living in a world where options are weighed in an Internet environment, they search for the right school with the same determination and care as shopping for a child-care provider, a vacation home, a new car. Choices abound, and Gen Xers see it as their job to do a thorough search.

Enter Park Street Elementary's baby boomer principal Mary Beth, born between 1948 and 1962 (Howe and Strauss, 2007). When Cassie e-mailed Mary Beth in detail about her search and to set up a meeting,

Mary Beth began to wonder: Is my parent-communication strategy stuck in a time warp? Am I competing effectively for potentially great students of tuned-in, caring parents?

American Generations
Name and Birth Years

- WW II 1901–1924
- Silent 1925–1942
- Boom 1943–1960
- Generation X 1961–1981
- Millennial 1982–2005
- Homeland 2005–2025

(Howe and Strauss, 2007)

WHO ARE THESE GEN XERS?

If Mary Beth's questions give you pause, they should. To get the attention of parents today, traditional print tools—such as newsletters, bulletins, and long prose documents—must be upgraded with electronic options, the Web and e-mail, and a writing style that is easy to skim and comprehend. Following are some other things we know about our Gen X parents.

Relationships

Gen X parents place great importance on the value of relationships. The quest for give and take and the desire for community are needs that must be met with warm, personal communication and an invitation to be a member of the team. Opportunities for group discussion are welcome, and e-mail and text messages that have the personal touch are not just read, but valued.

Options

Parents in this generation value options and seek custom solutions to their problems. Have two different programs for high school diplomas?

Hooray! Market the heck out of them and explain the pros and cons. Offer opportunities for discussion, questions, and firsthand looks. There's no such thing as too much good information. Make it clear and say it loud when you can provide custom solutions to individual circumstances. For example, an additional bus providing students transportation home from after-school activities, should be showcased as a benefit for parents. This message shows the school's willingness to work in partnership with parents to provide opportunities for children to succeed.

Authority

Generation X parents, as a group, often show indifference to rules and a general distrust of institutions and authority figures. It is important for school leaders to build relationships with parent groups at the first opportunity. These parents develop tremendous loyalty to what they believe in. Your job is to harness that energy and creativity to serve the greater school community. Find an effective way to raise important issues—the need for additional staff, a new auditorium, a new solution to the issue of student stress—and engage the parent community in its resolution. This is a generation of problem solvers who thrive on collaboration and accomplishment.

GETTING THE LAY OF THE LAND

Mary Beth decided to organize a focus group of parents. The report from this group confirmed her suspicion that today's parents reject the long-held ways that most schools use to communicate with them. For example, the newsletter she regarded as her signature communication vehicle was rejected by her parents as being too long and cumbersome. The way parents were greeted when they came into the school's front office was important, as was a strong desire to be considered a part of the school team.

Addressing the issue quickly, Mary Beth developed a new strategy grounded in understanding and meeting the expectations of Gen X parents. Her objective was to build parent relationships needed to meet her ultimate goal: student achievement. She targeted the parents of kindergartners and identified ways she could connect them to the school. To get a taste of what she did, let's take a look.

CREATING A VIRTUAL FIRST IMPRESSION

The parent focus group noted that her baby boomer timing for mail—snail mail, that is—was off because kindergarten information arrived in parents' homes just weeks before spring orientation. Gen X parents, however, have been browsing and blogging for months, sometimes years, searching for information. Spring is too late. Public schools compete with private schools, home schooling and child-care centers where enrollment decisions need to be made months before public school kindergarten registration. School talk starts way early among Gen Xers. Consider this 2005 e-mail she received from another father:

> My wife and I have a daughter born on June 12, 2004. She will be able to start school in 2009. We are expecting another daughter any day now. From what I know, she would normally have to start kindergarten in 2011 since she would be born in October. Considering we would like the children to be close in grades, is there any way for her to start kindergarten in 2010?

Shaking your head in disbelief? Gen Xers get it. Dad's e-mail request is well within their norm. Raised by ready information on demand, they create for themselves a new environment of choice that allows them to decide among wide choices and to expect individual solutions.

Principals must embrace the Internet as their communication tool to create a solid first impression with these Gen X parents. Failure to offer a dynamic website or to answer e-mail raises cautionary flags about the school's relevance in a wired world.

Thanks to Mary Beth's hard work, Gen X parents looking for information on Park Street Elementary now will not be disappointed. Any time, any day, parents can go to the school's website and find answers to their questions. The school's homepage offers a special link taking parents of preschoolers to a page of their own. Information on that page describes the kindergarten program, introduces teachers, and provides an opportunity for parent-school interaction via e-mail.

There's more. Dates for school tours are announced regularly, and parents are encouraged to visit. This September's tour is already booked with parents of next September's kindergarten class. That's not surprising.

Gen Xers in Midlife

They will set about fortifying their social environment. As many of them confront financial difficulties, they will take pride in their ability to "have a life" and to wall off their families from economic turmoil. Their divorce rate will be well below that of Boomers and Silents at the same age. They will be extremely protective of their offspring; large numbers will spend hard-earned money and may relocate to ensure the quality of their children's schools and the safety of their daily lives. As their children reach college age, Gen Xers will apply to every facet of higher education the same no-child-left-behind attitude they applied to K–12 education (Howe and Strauss, 2007).

USING THE TELEPHONE TO REACH OUT

Mary Beth understood that Gen X parents are sensitive to customer service. She realized that time and good will spent building an informative Internet presence can be quickly destroyed by an impatient, disinterested, or intimidating voice at the other end of a parental call to the front office. One of the focus group parents described turning to a private school after a telephone slight from the public one. "They told me to call back in six months," she said. "I wasn't about to wait."

If you don't take charge of the telephone, you'll spend more time mending the effects of a rude exchange than planning steps to help people do it right the first time. One customer service study estimates it takes sixteen friendly actions to repair one unfriendly encounter (Barlow and Moeller, 1996).

She started by pinpointing the right people. An office staffer who believes the parent world should be seen but not heard should not be answering the phone in your front office. Instead, look for a smart, patient voice that conveys a smile. The right combination of knowledge and affability sends the message you intend.

Mary Beth offered guidance and training to the staff. Changing the culture and working conditions for office staff requires thought and intention. The reculturing of Park Street's front office happened quickly once Mary Beth set the tone. The office staff quickly established new protocols that supported the principal's new vision.

Office staff members prepared consistent, concise, and cogent answers to commonly asked questions. Each parent call is now followed up by recording the parent's name and address into a database and mailing a postcard with the website address and a handwritten message of welcome.

Parent calls are an opportunity for the school to strut its stuff. Courteous, helpful responses and follow-up are critical pieces in making the project a success.

AFTER THE POSTCARDS, THE EVENTS

At Park Street Elementary, you'll see a strong investment in kindergarten orientation and registration events. The strategy is to reassure parents: we know what we're doing; we want you here; we love children.

Invitations to these events are accompanied by concise, bulleted information that anticipates questions and leads parents through the process. Jargon is replaced by clarity. The old focus on rules and regulations is gone. The new orientation is all about show and tell. Parents move around the building, meeting with the principal and kindergarten teachers as they experience their child's future routine.

A few weeks later, the parent returns to the school with his child for registration. A carefully choreographed experience starts from the time they walk into the school and are greeted in a clutter-free lobby. There's no waiting, because each parent and his child has been given an appointment time. From the sign-in table, parent and child are escorted through a circuit around the school. The first stop is a room where the school counselor is seated. After the child is comfortable, the parent leaves and moves on to meet with a school staff member who walks the parent through paper work. The child visits a kindergarten classroom in session. Parent and child are reunited in the library where refreshments accompany a friendly prescreening process. When the good-byes are exchanged, the children each receive a "goody bag" that includes a book. A school bus awaits, and parent and child are treated to a ride around the neighborhood block.

• • •

Note to boomers: The tables have turned. The generation gap you bemoaned with your parents' generation is back to haunt you. Generation

Xers are here and with them a communication style that requires attention and adaptation. The days of mailing a sixteen-page newsletter with expectations that it will be read or announcing a new dismissal schedule without parent input are over. Historical events and cultural influences have resulted in a new way we all approach public institutions. There is increasing pressure on all our parents to be wary and skeptical. Understanding this behavior is important to developing a strategy for school improvement through strong, long-lasting relationships with parents.

For reflection

1. Describe the generational demographics of your school staff, parent community, and community at large.
2. Consider a conflict the school has encountered with a parent. Explain how generational differences might have been at the root of the conflict.
3. Describe communications techniques you use or could use to reach Generation X parents.

ENGAGE THE COMMUNITY

Breaking Gridlock

We started off trying to set up a small anarchist community, but people wouldn't obey the rules.

—Alan Bennett

Demands for greater community participation in local education decision making have turned school culture on its ear. The strong, silent leader who governed with unquestioned authority is becoming a relic of the past. School administrators today must speak the language of community collaboration, partnership, and engagement. The ability of schools to educate all students depends on it.

But talk is easy. "Doing collaboration"—authentic collaboration—is not. What we see now is a gap between knowing and doing, a gap filled with well-intentioned efforts to court parent and community participation that merely dance around the edges of real collaboration. Often the conversation between school and community ends in gridlock:

- A school district survey asks for parent input on the grading scale and finds wide disagreement. Parents are then told, "Sorry, it's too late in the year to do anything about it."
- A school governance team is comprised only of administration supporters.

- Input is sought from parents on the sixth-grade graduation program. A decision had already been made.
- Opinions of staff members are solicited on a staff development program. Administrators react with defensive answers.
- Community satisfaction is polled in a districtwide survey. Results are not made public.

These practices, and others like them, illustrate fruitless attempts at collaboration with stakeholders. While they give a tip of the hat to community involvement, they lack the follow-through to make the exercise meaningful. Fostering a connected school environment comes with wholesale change driven by a new set of beliefs.

COMMUNITY INPUT IS KEY TO STUDENT SUCCESS

Leaders who authentically engage the community believe that the stubborn gaps in educating all children only are filled by including community and valuing the ideas they bring to the table. We're not talking lip service here. Instead, we're asking for open acknowledgment that the school's ideas alone are no longer enough.

Miami Dade County Superintendent Rudy Crew is such a believer. Heading the nation's fourth-largest school district, Crew's leadership embraces knowledge from all stakeholders, even those who vigorously challenge the status quo.

"A demanding parent," he says, "is an engaged parent." Learning how to hear and to value their knowledge is a leadership function; the connections that result are critical to student success."

Believing that it is the school's obligation to market this fundamental belief, Miami-Dade developed a branding campaign that educates the community about the give-and-take process of education. A district tagline promises to "give students the world." Subsequent messages describe what "it takes," to make the tagline real. Small posters and giant signs on the sides of buildings grace downtown Miami, telling the school story through headlines and pictures. *It takes . . . collaboration; It takes . . . courage; It takes . . . commitment.*

Through these awareness efforts, the superintendent opened the door, inviting all to participate in conversations about the community's children. The school system plays host.

As Crew talks about the long-term value of engagement, especially in creating trust, he pulls from his shirt pocket small cards on which he had written details from chance meetings with community members. He read from one note about a man he met who wondered if the schools could make use of his donation of a boat that was in need of repair.

"At this point, I don't know how or what we'll do with it, but I guarantee we'll figure out a productive use for that boat," Crew said.

Validating the value of stakeholder interest by taking follow-up action is what effective leadership in school engagement looks like.

But, you may say, what if we really can't make use of the boat or any other gift or idea you may find whacky? Ignoring or rejecting such offers out of hand tells the stakeholder that their gesture is not valued. Instead, keep the focus on our next key belief, the value of nurturing relationships.

AUTHENTIC ENGAGEMENT IS A PROCESS

Successful school-community engagement resembles a courtship where relationship-building precedes a bended knee proposal. A fruitful courtship starts with simple questions (where were you born?) and progresses over time to more difficult ones (how many children would you like to have?). Asking the serious question on the first date may be reason enough to end the relationship.

The same thinking applies to school division attempts at stakeholder courtship. You can't start too big. The role of the leader is to tread carefully and incrementally, manage the small steps of relationships and make adjustments along the way.

One school system was anxious to engage the community in developing a long-range strategic plan. They started by inviting community members to work with school board members to develop a vision. People from a variety of locations and backgrounds were gathered together, seated at round tables and given pens and pads of lined paper. One school board member was stationed at each table, armed with a felt-tip marker and large pieces of newsprint. School board member to group: "OK. Let's talk about the hopes and dreams you have for your children. I'll write your answers up here." Huh?

Efforts at community engagement, like this one, often fail at the starting line because of questions that were simply too big. Asking stakeholders to define the school vision, for example, is not a good first date question. Beginning with questions that require people to talk explicitly about their hopes and dreams rarely works. Sure, a vision statement is written, but the interactive process so valuable to the effort is lost.

Rather than making the first move with questions about affairs of high moment, start with issues that are small and safe, something like:

- Creating a plan to select members for a parent advisory committee.
- Developing guidelines for a staff in-service program.
- Collecting teacher strategies for grading homework.

Tangible issues are safe starters; discussion of them is less threatening. The process is more important than the topic. The first outcome is learning to demonstrate mutual respect and personal regard. No detail is too small.

Engagement Circle

Think of topics related to your school's vision as being contained in a circle. Write them down. Then, record topics related to your community's vision in a second circle. Determine where the two circles intersect. There you'll find the topic on which you can begin the engagement conversation. The overlapping part of the circles symbolizes what you have in common and provides a point of strength to begin collaboration.

ENGAGE FROM THE GROUND UP

Tommy T, a principal at a large suburban high school, makes a point of learning as many parent names as possible. He knows the power of greeting people by name and connecting them to their children. He builds relationships from the smallest level.

Tommy knows that conversations have the power to transform a culture, and that he can't have meaningful conversations with people he doesn't know or who don't know him. Tommy is a leader who creates a compelling picture of the future and involves others fully in managing genuine change. It all starts when he learns their names.

When a group of parents began an organized lobbying effort to change the school's starting time to later in the morning, Tommy embraced the group (after all, he knew them by name) and with them created a committee made up of those from all sides of the issue. They agreed on clear operational expectations. The committee members effectively built relationships, framed the issues, explained the facts (including costs, bus schedule complexity, and conflicting research) and made a report to the school board. Everyone had been treated fairly, no one was made to be wrong, and the school board voted—against changing the starting time. Yet, all on the committee had dinner together afterward. Smart leadership can produce progressive engagement, but remember where it started: small acts, like knowing people's names.

Another school system spent long hours and many months reacting to a group of parents lobbying on the same issue. The school's response to hearing the group's rumblings was "ignore and maybe they'll go away." It didn't work. Tensions rose, walls went up and the issue remains unresolved. Many thousands of dollars in school resources were wasted and no partnerships were built. For that system, the issue has never gone away.

Community Engagement as a Contact Sport

School leaders who are upfront and openly communicate expectations for community engagement put themselves at an advantage. It's a give and take process that involves holding the line on some issues and pushing the envelope on others. Engaging community members in the process of drawing that line is an important first step.

PAYING ATTENTION TO YOUR COMMUNITY

It may seem like a good idea to conduct a poll of your community. After all, poll results can tell you what your community thinks about the school and what they'd like to see happen in the future. We advise caution. Major pitfalls congregate around these questions:

- Are you prepared to publish the results?
- Are you prepared to actively address issues the community raises?
- Are you prepared to make a significant financial investment in designing a statistically accurate survey?

If you can't answer yes to each of these questions, you may not be far enough along in the engagement business to benefit from a formal survey. The problem is that although the poll is a tool that can be used to great advantage at a later stage in the listening process, effective two-way communication at much lower levels of risk is a better building block. School communication has a long tradition of being one-way—newsletters, telephone reminders, flyers, websites, report cards. When information comes the other way, especially in the form of disagreement, suggestions, or questions to authority, it requires a new communication skill set to address.

One school board tested the engagement waters in a costly survey on community satisfaction with their schools. The community's negative response to one question was enough to plunge the results into a black hole. No one ever talked about the survey again. The question that sank the survey ship: Rate the effectiveness of your school board member. Ouch!

Informal Surveys

Informal surveys—shorter and tightly focused on one topic are an alternative to the comprehensive formality of the longer model. Typically ten questions or fewer, what they lack in statistical validity is made up for in their ability to take the community temperature more quickly. One way to start is a feedback card before and after an event.

One school used such a short survey to prepare for back-to-school night. Parents were asked to evaluate several features of previous years' events. Staff then used the information from the survey to prepare for the next back-to-school night. Following the event, parents were asked to complete another feedback survey. Those results were made available in the parent newsletter and were the subject of discussion at a staff meeting. Simply offering parents the opportunity to express an opinion about the event changed the paradigm and set the stage for further two-way dialogue.

Focus Groups

Linda, a third-year principal at a large high school who, was looking for a way to increase involvement levels, turned to a focus group, a small gathering of people who were led in discussion by a facilitator trained to promote genuine interaction. Linda offered staff members the opportunity to train as a facilitator with the stipulation that they would then conduct the parent groups.

Linda wisely limited the scope of the focus group discussion to one topic, which happened to be communication, an area that she had evidence was a real concern. Over the past few months, parent e-mails had indicated dissatisfaction about the communication between home and school, particularly around the timing of when information was sent. This was a relatively low-risk, specific issue that everyone could easily understand. The topic was "engage-able" and one that could improve the quality of life for both parents and teachers.

Three focus groups of parents were organized and conducted by staff members. These staff members then reported results to the rest of the staff in small group meetings. Starting with positive parent comments, they went on to report parental complaints about last-minute notifications and the impact it had on their ability to participate and support their children. Understanding things from this new perspective struck a sympathetic chord, and staff members outlined new practices. An article in the school newsletter followed, and the conversation continued. Parents were enthusiastic participants in the process and were grateful for having been asked and engaged on the issue.

Take note that the lack of timeliness in home-school communication was not resolved through a list of rules. It was solved as a result of people coming together and learning to appreciate one another's points of view. It was a discussion of values and beliefs under the guise of timeliness. It was resolved as a result of question asking, listening, and then "Oh . . . I see now. I understand how my actions can make your life better."

The focus group establishes a question-asking process that has the power to challenge the status quo culture of every school community. Simply asking for opinions gets us off the dime. Value is added by listening to the answer and responding.

Listening Savvy

Law of human nature: all of us are annoying to a certain degree. Unfortunately, we rarely acknowledge it or change. The smart leader listens, learns, and looks for new strategies for better relationship building.

For example, one superintendent described how she learned through listening and observing two members of a high-level committee who liked to pick at details and find fault. Instead of trying to cut the naysayers off, apologize, or ignore them, the superintendent started discussions of thorny issues by inviting them to tell what they regarded as pitfalls. Eventually, all, including the nitpickers were able to chuckle at their foible. The powerful message from the superintendent's behavior was that she was on to them *and* willing to appreciate them, warts and all. Standing in a defensive posture, responding in kind or ignoring them would have multiplied the annoyances and taken the committee on a very different path. Lesson: sophisticated listening savvy is central to a leader's survival and a flourishing school system.

• • •

Many school leaders have incorporated procedures to offer opportunities for community dialogue, but others are wary. Some think they can't afford the time it takes. Others worry that they are opening the virtual can of worms. Yet, with focus and leadership, two-way communication opens fruitful discussions and building relationships that support school strength and student success.

For reflection

1. What procedures do you have or plan on developing that engage the community in small ways?
2. Find a media article that involves conflict between citizens and a government agency (preferably a school). Speculate on the origin of the conflict and how it might relate to lack of leadership.
3. How can teachers develop leadership skills to engage challenging students in productive ways?

II

THE FRAMEWORK

DESIGN YOUR OFFENSE

Engaging Stakeholders to Drive Achievement

When I see a thick manual, I know I am looking at a slow company.

—Tom Peters

The call to our office almost always came too late.

"We're ready to roll out the plan for the new parent education center. Can you help us communicate it?"

"Our parents are really upset with the stories in the media about the dismissal of our food service worker. Can you help?"

Communication at its best happens on the front end of events, not after the horses have left the barn. To put communication up front means thinking ahead. For new programs and projects, it means making communication part of the original scheme. For building good relationships with all stakeholders and for the general health of the organization, it means devising and implementing a year-round, schoolwide or division-wide communications plan—*before* someone steps on a landmine.

We have always maintained that you never see our best work: it is what we do ahead of time to *prevent* the firestorm. Use good communication to keep yourself out of trouble, so you don't have to use it to mop up the mess!

A communication plan can be as simple or as detailed as you choose to make it. For short-term events, chances are you will make a simple plan. For building long-term community support for a capital bond issue or for the introduction of a new superintendent, a more detailed structure may be called for. Whatever communication you have to do and whatever kind of a plan you choose to use, there are key questions to ask and key elements to include.

WHY PLAN? WHAT DOES IT BUY ME?

It is no stretch to say that the time and energy invested in an up-front communication plan is only an investment of enlightened self-interest for you and your team.

- A strong communication plan gives you a good road map. It allows you to focus efforts and resources on your project from the beginning. You don't get diverted into extraneous, and potentially expensive, activities. A timeline keeps everyone on task.
- Early messages to your stakeholders offer you opportunities to talk about a new project or the coming school year in the context of your shared vision and mission.
- Proactive communication strategies set stakeholders' expectations. At the outset you are able to say clearly what the program can and cannot achieve, significantly reducing your clients' potential disappointments.
- Good planning, with built-in reality checks along the way, can anticipate problems and solve them before they appear.
- A good communication plan establishes your accountability to your stakeholders, and it gives you a reason to say "no" to requests for activities or events that don't move you toward the goal.

In one study (Grunig, 2002), corporate CEOs with excellent communication programs reported a 225% return on their investment in public relations.

WHAT IS A COMMUNICATION PLAN?

The best communication plan is a framework of goals and strategies by which leadership can:

- Disseminate information about a specific program or about the school or school division
- Build supportive, collaborative relationships with stakeholders
- Influence the behavior of those stakeholders on behalf of the organization

The best plans are based on research that identifies the various stakeholders who will be influenced by the program and what they believe. These plans are built with participation from representatives of both those who will carry out the plan and those for whom the communication is intended. The best plans are *market tested* before they are launched. They are *flexible* enough to be changed. The best plans include an *evaluation* component and measurable goals. These plans are the product of *strategic thinking*.

Sound complicated already? It can be, but it doesn't have to be. Here is the communication plan that Glenhurst Elementary School designed to communicate the new school vision and goals to the school community.

A committee of faculty and parents first worked together to clarify what they considered the most important messages about their new vision. Then they listed their chief stakeholders: staff members, parents, students, members of the neighboring community. For this team and this plan, these four groups were enough. These were their most important target audiences.

To identify the messages that they wanted to send to each group, the Glenhurst team asked the questions:

- How will this new plan affect each group?
- What will individuals in each group want to hear about the plan?
- How much will each group want to hear? (Clearly, faculty members needed more specifics about the school plan than the neighbors did.)

Table 6.1. Communication Plan

Key Messages about Our Initiative

1.
2.
3.

STAKEHOLDER	MESSAGE(S) (How does this affect you?)	MEDIUM(S) (How do you want to hear the message?)	EVALUATION TOOL (How do I know that you understand)	RELATIONSHIP (How can we build a strong relationship?)
Staff members				
Parents				
Students				
Community				

Name of Initiative:

Start Date:

Completion Date:

The team then decided how they would get the messages to each of the groups.

- Who uses e-mail?
- Who uses the website?
- What groups needed to meet the principal face-to-face?
- With whom could they use large group sessions?

The team talked about the need to send their messages repeatedly to each group, using as many means as was practicable. More than one media was listed for each group.

To add an evaluative component, the team asked themselves:

- How will we know that each group understands?
- What behavior will each group exhibit once they "get" the messages? (More parent volunteer hours? More staff participation in future planning sessions?)

Again, for each stakeholder group, the team listed a number of indicators.

Finally, the group asked: How can we use this new school plan and our communication to build stronger relationships with each of these stakeholders? They talked about the kinds of relationships they already had with each stakeholder group and charted what effort they would need to extend for each group.

They wrote out their plan, using one page per stakeholder group. And then they went to work.

WHAT ARE THE KEY ELEMENTS OF A GOOD PLAN?

The Glenhurst plan provided that school community with a great way to launch their new school plan. If your project is more elaborate, your communication plan may also include more moving parts. Here is a look at what those parts might be:

a. *Mission.* At the top of your plan, you need to state clearly, in no more than three sentences, what it is you want to communicate. You need to be clear about where you are going.

"The goal is to introduce and build support for the new districtwide bus and walker safety campaign."

"The goal is to provide employees, parents, and members of the community information about, and to encourage support for, the new instructional programs outlined in the superintendent's budget."

"The goal is to convince this community that Woburn Middle School is providing all students an excellent education and teaching them skills for life in the twenty-first century."

b. *Research*. This component can stop you for years if you let it. That would be a mistake. Most people don't do any research at all and ride on their assumptions. That is also a mistake. Find a middle ground. Do what researchers call an "environmental" or a "cultural" scan. How does your community feel about this issue? How does information travel fastest in your community? Are there informal networks you need to tap? Who can be an effective spokesperson for the issue? Ask questions of your stakeholders and listen. Focus groups work too. Or use an online survey. Sometimes the research has already been done. Did someone else already ask the question? Are there survey results you can use?

c. *Audiences*. As the Glenhurst team did, you should identify who will be affected by your project and/or who you want to reach with your messages. Glenhurst identified parents, employees, students, and community. You may wish to add categories: elected officials, senior citizens, neighborhood associations, conservation associations, the Latino community, religious leaders, the media, parents of preschoolers, or alumni/ae, all depending on your project.

d. *Assumptions*. All too often we begin a project with assumptions about our audiences that are wrong. We think we know what they know or understand. We think we know what they *should* know and forget to ask what they *want* to know. We also think we know how to best reach these audiences. We say, "We created a brochure and put it out on the counter, therefore everyone knows." Or "I send out a newsletter once a week. That's pretty good communication, right?" Schools are surprised to find that the reason parents don't show up at school is not because they are not interested, but because they did not get the message or be-cause they don't feel welcome. A quick check of what we are as-suming can keep us from making mistakes. Make a list.

e. *Messages*. Even though the instructional program you are intro-ducing may have many moving parts, your communication mes-sages must be simple: "We are winners." "We put kids first." "This plan makes us accountable." Different audiences may want to hear different messages about the same program—and in differ-ent amounts of detail.

f. *Delivery systems*. The delivery system must match the audience. Gen X parents don't read long, printed newsletters. They want their information on the Web. Stay-at-home moms trade a lot of information over morning coffee. Faculties comfortable with e-mail and the Web hate long, informational faculty meetings. Re-tirees, on the other hand, may read every word you send them.

g. *Time lines*. Glenhurst did not put a time line in their first plan. They could have added an action plan later. Clear deadlines for task com-pletion is a great way to be sure the work is staying on track.

h. *Responsible person or department*. The way to really be sure that things get done is to put the right person in charge. Spreading the responsibility for a program also increases the number of people who have investment in the success of the initiative.

i. *Available resources*. This is another key piece of the action plan. It does no good to design posters with the new school motto if there is no money for printing. Before you launch a campaign, best to know what it will cost. Be sure to include all the costs nec-essary for success. Being clear about program fiscal needs at the beginning of the project helps set the agenda and saves you the frustration of having to quit halfway down the road.

j. *Evaluation*. We evaluate in order to make our programs better. We need to ask, "What changed as a result of our communica-tion?" And, "Was this project a good return on our investment?" Measuring progress throughout the project is what you need to do. Ask people. Create simple surveys. Watch your Web traffic. Did your message get through?

Somewhere in your planning, you and your team may want to take a longer look at the unintended opportunities and consequences that this communication effort may offer you. If you sign on a particular elected official who likes to talk about the topic, you may have built a relationship that can help you in other ways. On the other hand, what problems are you are likely to encounter as you launch your communication? Who are the people who are likely to react negatively to your efforts? Who could be offended by your messages?

In our office, we began every communication initiative with newsprint and markers and an hour dedicated just to thinking out loud together about all these issues. If you make newsprint a habit in your office, you will find that with practice you can come away pretty quickly with the outline of a plan.

WHO MAKES THE PLAN?

If you are planning a districtwide initiative and your school district has a communication office, those are the folks who should lead the charge. If you are a principal wanting to tout your new school renovation, your team should come from within your school community. If a member of the district communication office will agree to be part of that team, you can harness their expertise as well.

In any case, having stakeholders sit on the committee is a must. Planning a ground breaking for a new school? Include representatives from the architectural firm, the facilities department, the parent community, the new staff (if there is one yet), and the community at large on the planning team. Stay in touch with the school board and other elected officials who may want to come as well. This is what we would call in the office an "All Skate" occasion!

If the planning team gets too large, you may need a working group to hammer out the details and report back to the larger team. But having all those groups on board from the start will assure a successful event.

SOME NOTES ON TACTICS

Tactics are the part that everyone loves. You get to do stuff. These are the specific activities that will carry your messages out. Everyone has their favorite tactics—usually the ones they themselves do well. But choose wisely. Be strategic. Focusing the efforts of your team on a few, well-chosen tactics and doing them well is the best move.

Some years ago, Fairfax County Public Schools consolidated half of its central office staff from a number of buildings spread across the county into a single facility. The move involved several hundred people (Fairfax County is a big system). It also left several hundred other employees out in old offices, waiting for the second building to be built. A large committee with representatives from all the departments being moved and several that were not moving but were essential to the move (like Facilities and Information Technology) met regularly for over a year to plan the details of the move *and* to design the communication of the move.

As time went on, it became clear that, of all the potential stakeholder audiences, the folks who were most interested and most involved were the employees who were moving. The school board only wanted to know that we were on time and on budget. Other central office employees slated to move to the second building only wanted to know when their building would be ready. Staff members and parents in schools only needed to be reassured that services to their schools would not be interrupted during the move.

So the committee and the communications office focused on the moving employees. To calm their fears, these folks needed reliable information as quickly as it was available, so our first focus was on the website. The site carried artist renderings of the new building, pictures and video of the construction, information about paint and carpet colors, how to use the new telephone system, how to pack your files, where to find the packing boxes, and how to mark them. There was a Q&A section that dispelled rumors (and there were many) as soon as they surfaced. Any employee could access this information at any time—even from home.

The site was thorough, updated regularly, and well used. Because it was successful (we tracked the hits), we decided to print only a few, specifically targeted brochures and pamphlets, mostly for external audiences.

As the time drew closer to the move, and the building was safe for visitors, the committee organized a series of staggered visits, over a two-day period, for the new occupants. Transportation provided big yellow school buses to move the employees from their offices to the new building. Food services served coffee and cookies in the new cafeteria. Each department "decorated" their still cavernous and unfinished spaces with

crepe paper and balloons. The office sizes were marked out on the concrete floors so that employees could have a sense of what their space
would feel like. There were demonstrations of the new telephone technology. Everyone was greeted at the door and welcomed to their new
"home." The event turned into a party. People left with smiles on their
faces.

These two tactics—the website and the visits—became the center-
pieces for the communication during that year. Evaluations indicated
that staff members felt informed and were happy to have a preview of
their surroundings. Moving days—they were also staggered—went
smoothly. The boxes were delivered to the right rooms and, for the most
part, the computers worked when they were booted up. The move was
big. The communication was big. Planning was what made it work.

Especially if your communication campaign is a long one, note that
your tactics may change as time goes on. You may begin distributing
your messages widely through press releases, e-mail newsletters, and
your website to alert a broad audience. As time goes on, however, you
may want to focus more on a smaller, more highly affected group of
stakeholders, much as we did with the central office move. On the other
hand, you may want to start a bond campaign, for instance, with meetings of smaller groups of key communicators who will then help you
carry your message to a wider audience. In that case, the bumper stickers and the banners come later.

A FINAL NOTE ON MESSAGES

When you sit down to map out your communication scheme, you may
find that you have many messages you would like to take to your audiences. It takes a lot of discipline to narrow the key messages to *three* or
two or even just *one*! You have to prioritize. Remember that you are
competing for space in your stakeholder's brain in a world that broad-
casts thousands of messages everyday. There's not much room on the
airwaves. One terrific message repeated over and over again in many
formats ("Bayer Aspirin: expect wonders," for instance) is better than
five well-documented arguments laid out in four-color glossy splendor.
What *is* you message?

WHERE DO YOU STORE THE PLAN?

Communication plans are not for the shelf. They must be working documents, marked up, erased, changed constantly. And when the project is completed, it's done! What you carry forward to your next project is the *process* and, with any luck, the newly strengthened goodwill of your community. Next time, you build on that. The next time you will have a new team, a new project, and new messages. You must start your planning all over again.

We strongly recommended that every school district have an overarching communication plan or framework within which each school and department can work and to which all messages in the district can be tied. The more internal cohesion your stakeholders feel in your organization—consciously or unconsciously—the stronger the relationship you can build with them. Don't confuse parents and community people with a plethora of logos and slogans.

Our communities, like our parents, do not want to be spun. They want honest information in a timely fashion. They want us to show them how we are educating their children. They want to hear our stories. A good plan can help you do just that.

• • •

Whether you are drawing up a simple communication plan to support the fall book fair or a broader plan to support districtwide communication for the school year, you and your team need to incorporate your communication efforts into the project planning from the very beginning. A communication plan is a road map to help focus resources and efforts. It is a great tool to identify and manage stakeholder expectations from the start. It can also save you the time and frustration of heading down a dead-end road.

For reflection

1. Does your school/district need a new communication plan?
2. Name three new projects that should include a communication plan.
3. Who could best help you create a communication plan?
4. Who are your key audiences?
5. What are the best delivery systems available for your messages?
6. What are the first three steps you should take to develop a communication plan?

HARNESS YOUR SECRET WEAPON

Communicating Effectively
with Colleagues and Employees

We generally do better work when we know what the hell we're doing and why the hell we're doing it.

—Carville and Begala

Meaning is what motivates people.

—Margaret J. Wheatley

In his study of Dwight Eisenhower as general, John Wukovitz (2006),
military historian and former eighth-grade history and language arts
teacher, attempts to draw lessons in leadership that anyone can use.
From Eisenhower's career, he teases out leadership principles that he
believes were essential to the general's success. Among those principles
Wukovitz identified are "The team comes first" and "Take care of your
men."

Eisenhower liked to leave the office and get into the field as often as
he could. According to Wukovitz, the general made a habit of talking to
soldiers, individually and in small groups, and, in doing so, Eisenhower
"linked them into a great enterprise."

"The basis for leadership," says Jeswald Salacuse, professor of law at
the Fletcher School of Law and Diplomacy, Tufts University (2006), "is

your relationship with the persons you lead. Trust in the leader is a necessary element of leadership, and persons are more disposed to follow a leader in whom they have trust than one they do not trust. *Communication is your fundamental tool in building those relationships*" (p. 15, italics added).

Effective school leaders understand the power of trust, either intuitively or from on-the-job experience, and they are intentional in their cultivation of that trust with their employees. There are a number of very compelling reasons why they pay attention.

EMPLOYEES MAKE CHANGE HAPPEN

The relationships that a school leader builds with staff members throughout the organization undergird the success—or failure—of any program or initiative. (Remember how the superintendent we mentioned in the introduction carried his customer service message out to his employees in person? He did not rely on memos. He talked directly with the troops.) In today's world, to remain strong, a school or school district must be able to grow and change. To sustain change over time, an organization must develop the ability to be flexible. What allows an organization to develop that flexibility and remain flexible through change and uncertainty is the strength of the relationships and the trust that has been developed among the people who work in that organization.

Think of the principals or superintendents who have come into your neighborhood and successfully made sweeping changes in a short time. Each one has had a clear vision and a plan, but each one has also been able quickly to gain the trust of people deep in the organization. Whether the goal is raising test scores or reorganizing pay-grade structures, the key is always the relationships.

EMPLOYEES CAN BE A POWERFUL MARKETING FORCE

Employees also have the potential to be a school's or a school division's most effective marketing tool. Fairfax County Public Schools (FCPS) is one of Virginia's largest employers—over 20,000 employees, teachers and support staff. Our mantra to *all* the leaders throughout the school system was this: "If everyone in FCPS were spreading the good news about our schools in the community, we could have the largest marketing force in the state!" That includes not just teachers but bus drivers, food service workers, administrative aides, electricians, and supply officers!

Unfortunately, in most school districts not every employee speaks well of the school system. Not every employee feels a part of the organization or invested in its success. The conversations those employees hold at church or at the gas pump can be very damaging.

One day, we were standing at the checkout counter of a local grocery store. Behind us, two twenty-somethings were chatting animatedly about their workplace—the local hospital. It seems they both worked in the hospital's critical care unit, and both were very unhappy.

"I watch the mistakes they make with the IVs and meds every day," one said.

"No one seems to care," the other replied. "No one checks up."

This was meant to be a private conversation between two employees, but it was damaging because the allegations were totally uncorroborated and the conversation was held in a public place within earshot of at least a dozen other customers pushing grocery carts, any or all of whom could have been potential clients of the hospital—or donors! The allegations were being made by insiders—the people who should know what's going on. Other people were listening.

The same kinds of conversations about schools take place in grocery stores all across America when parents encounter teachers or other school employees. At that same grocery store where we were, a well-liked instructional assistant from a nearby elementary school works the checkout part-time. Every day, she sees parents and grandparents of the children in her school. If she were unhappy about her school or her teaching job, imagine the potential for damage.

Employees of an organization are perceived to have insider (informed) views of that organization. Research shows that generally teachers' opinions about a school are more highly regarded by parents and citizens than those of the principal, the superintendent, or members of the school board (Hunter, 2005). True or not, employee perceptions carry great weight.

SATISFIED EMPLOYEES MEANS SATISFIED PARENTS

Another reason that your relationship with your employees is critical to success is that the satisfaction of your customers (that is, your parents and your community) is directly related to the satisfaction of your employees. The well-being of your staff members—or lack thereof—is reflected in how they treat the students, parents, volunteers, and business partners with whom they work. It is, as we have already said, reflected in the conversations they hold in the grocery store!

A parent comes storming into a classroom after school, charging the teacher with neglect and incompetence. Is the teacher patient and polite? Or does the teacher dismiss the parent, pack up his briefcase, and leave—leaving a bigger mess? That may depend on the teacher's relationship with the building principal.

A group of neighbors comes to the district's facilities manager's office, demanding that the proposal for a cell tower to be erected at the back of the football field be taken off the table. Does the facilities manager find an appropriate way to hear and discuss the issue or does she refuse the meeting, sending the citizens to the local papers for airtime? The manager's response may be prompted by how much respect she feels the facilities department receives within the larger organization.

In large measure, our employees treat their colleagues and their stakeholders in the same way in which they feel they are being treated by their employer. When employees are treated with respect and feel valued by their organization, they will be more likely to treat their customers with equal respect. Disgruntled employees rarely care about how customers feel about the organization.

"There is concrete evidence that satisfied employees make for satisfied customers (and satisfied customers can in turn reinforce employees' sense of satisfaction in their job)," concludes Dr. Valarie Zeithaml, associate dean at UNC Kenan-Flagler Business School (Zeithaml and Bitner, 1996, pp. 304–5), who has done leading research in the field.

Zeithaml describes what she calls the "emotional labor" that it takes to keep an organization humming. Emotional labor includes "delivering smiles, making eye contact, showing sincere interest, and engaging in friendly conversation" with people who may be strangers. It is, she says, the "front line employees who shoulder this responsibility for the organization" (1996, pp. 307–8). In order to get your staff members to do the emotional labor of your organization day after day, you must be sure that they themselves feel a part of your team.

This leadership job is not getting easier. If—as we argue elsewhere in this book—leaders must now accommodate Generation X parents coming to our schools with their young children, leaders must also understand that the even younger generation of Millennials, who are showing up in the workplace, provide a whole new set of challenges to a very staid school industry. Questions of "What's in it for me?" replace, or at least accompany, the older, traditional questions of "How can I fit into this organization?" Hold on—we are in for another paradigm shift in communication and employee relationships.

GET THE TROOPS ENGAGED

Whether you are the new superintendent in a school system or a successful principal who has been at the school for many years but now needs to make some course corrections, what you are asking your staff members to do is to trust you, to share your vision, and to learn some new ways.

There are some nonnegotiable conditions necessary for people to learn and grow, says teacher and consultant Margaret J. Wheatley (2005, p. 152), who has worked for more than thirty years in organizations and communities:

- People must understand and value your (the leader's) objective or strategy and understand how their work adds value to that objective.
- People must feel respected and trusted themselves within the organization.
- People must value and trust their leader.

Hard to make that happen if you are not taking care of the troops.

The bottom line is that you have to talk to your employees, engage them in the mission of the schools, and empower them to get the job done well. You have to make them feel like a worthwhile part of the enterprise.

A school board we once knew decided to spend time rethinking the vision and strategic goals of the division. For over a year, they met regularly with outside education consultants, working long hours and consuming many pounds of newsprint. They were diligent in their pursuit of the perfect framework for the school district.

Trouble was they worked in private. They closeted themselves away, never sharing their plans with their stakeholders, never asking their staff to contribute in any meaningful way to the process. The product was neatly crafted and coherent. But when it was presented to the parents in the district, few had any interest in what the school board had produced. Worse yet, when the school board asked the district's employees to use their vision and framework to shape the day-to-day operation of the schools, the employees could find little connection between what the board had written and their work on the front lines. The lack of communication with the troops during the creation process left the document effectively dead on arrival.

ENCOURAGE EFFECTIVE STAFF COMMUNICATION

FCPS (2005) did a study to try to understand why some teachers stayed in their jobs and why some transferred to other schools or left the district entirely. What incentives keep a teacher in a particular school? Is salary a key factor? Does teaching economically disadvantaged or language-minority children require combat pay? The study results offered some surprising insights.

Among the factors rated highest among teachers *who stayed in their school* were:

- Spirit of teamwork within the team and at the school
- Support from the administration
- Feedback, recognition, and caring from the administrative team
- Pride in working at the school and a sense that their work could make an impact on student achievement
- Overall management of the school

In other words, good leadership, a vision, and good communication.

There are lots of tools that principals and superintendents can use to talk with their employees. They are little different than those you use to develop ties with parents or community members. In some ways it is easier to connect with staff members, because the lines should already be open. Employees expect communication.

Technology has made it possible to reach large numbers of employees in a building or across a school division quickly, but, just as in politics (see chapter 3 on persuasion), you have to balance written communication with hands-on, face-to-face contact.

You must also encourage people to talk creatively with each other—not just to you. The reality today is that life is too complicated for any one person to have all the answers. It does require a team—and you have to empower the team to get to work.

IT HAS TO BE TWO-WAY

Over and over, what school leaders forget, or fail to understand, in their quest to communicate is that effective leadership requires regular, embedded feedback and response systems for their employees. Leaders also need to listen. Communication is not just about telling stuff. It is a two-way process.

On the night before the D-Day invasion of Normandy in World War II, General Eisenhower left headquarters and the company of his generals to go out into the night. He drove to a nearby airfield to talk with the troops of the 101st Airborne Division—a group of men slated to take 70 percent casualties the following day. It was his reality check. Principals and superintendents need to walk the building, not only to talk to students (although that is plenty important), but also to talk earnestly and often with staff members.

Every school leader has his or her own style of collecting wisdom from the troops. One principal we know created a spreadsheet listing every teacher's name. With a small notebook in hand, he dropped by several teachers' classrooms each week before or after school. On the spreadsheet he kept a record of his conversations, the teachers' needs, and the success stories they told. He used those conversations to shape his work.

And while you are out "on the street," remember to thank members of your staff for the good work they have done. Be specific about how they have contributed to the mission. A superintendent we know makes a habit of writing a short note every morning to a staff member who has gone above and beyond or to one who needs a boost. Some principals use faculty meetings to recognize good work. But even just saying a genuine thank you when you're in the halls means a lot.

School leaders use technology to take the temperature of the building or department—soliciting e-mail correspondence, employing simple Web surveys, or setting up internal bulletin boards for postings and Web conversations. One superintendent disciplined himself to visit every school in his very large district on a regular basis, often eating lunch in the cafeteria. Another held regular, small "town meetings" at the central office, to which any staff person in the district could come and talk.

Whatever means you choose, the important thing is that you start, that you are consistent in your efforts, and that you let your employees know when and how they can reach you. *And,* it is important to let employees see that you have used—or at least carefully considered—the advice you have gotten from them. Worse than not asking for opinions is asking and then ignoring the responses.

KEEP THE CLIMATE CIVIL

Nothing stops communication faster than rudeness, sarcasm, or intimidation. "That kind of behavior doesn't happen in my organization," you say. Of course, no one is rude to you—you are the chief. But look again.

We first identified this issue of incivility in the workplace in customer service workshops we conducted for front-office staff, who regularly interface with other staff members, parents, and members of the public. The stories these women (and they were mostly women) told of screaming, profanity, and threats were chilling. It reminded us of some of the most unpleasant calls that come to the superintendent's office.

We began asking questions of the other support service employees we encountered in our seminars—electricians who enter a classroom during the day to fix the lights or deliverymen bringing goods to the front office. We found that they had stories too. So did the people in human resources and technology. Even teachers talked about being bullied by parents, or other teachers, or the department head. Almost everyone could name someone in their building whose ugly behaviors they tried to avoid.

Was this a hostile organization that we worked in? No, in many ways, the climate was better than in some other systems we know. But there was an undercurrent of unpleasant behavior and—even more troublesome—we found that employees, particularly those at the bottom of the food chain, felt helpless to do anything about it.

Signs of Incivility
   Be on the lookout for complaints about employees who routinely:

   Threaten
   Insult
   Tease mercilessly
   Send caustic e-mails
   Ignore
   Intimidate
   Shame publicly
   Display raw anger

In recent years, incivility in the workplace has become a well-defined and studied problem. Schools are not the only place where people are rude and abusive. Incivility costs businesses millions of dollars a year in employee stress, distraction, absenteeism, turnover, and legal fees. One company figured that the extra cost for one "jerk" for one year—the street name is TCJ, total cost of jerk—for replacing the assistants the employee fired, the legal costs for the suits that ensued, and anger-management training for the employee was over $160,000 (Sutton, 2007).

A 2007 report by the nonprofit National Commission on Teaching and America's Future estimates that teacher turnover in U.S. school systems costs more than $7 billion a year. According to the report, nationally about 50 percent of teachers leave their jobs within their first five years. Most systems, the report adds, underestimate what the costs of these losses are.

At the same time, the press is reporting emerging research that suggests that teacher absences lead to lower student test scores—whether those absences are for a day or two or because the teacher has left the school or the system (Associated Press, 2008). To be sure, there are many reasons why teachers are not in their classrooms, but the stress of incivility is certainly one of them. The costs of incivility in our industry—both in terms of employee retention and student achievement—are largely hidden, but they are probably high.

"Increasing aggression is having a profound impact on organizational relationships. . . . More employees are retreating into self-protective stances, hording resources and information for fear of losing further control of their work. And worker stress levels are at an all-time high, as frequently reported in the popular press. It's now estimated that one third of lost days in Canada, England and the United States are due to worker stress" (Wheatley, 2005, p. 183).

Combating Incivility
    Set an example of civility.
    Codify workplace practices that display mutual respect.
    Enforce "no jerk" standards.
    Hire people with good attitudes.
    Teach constructive confrontation techniques.

Incivility is contagious. It is the leader's job to keep the organization free of the ridicule, demeaning comments, and silent stares that lead to employee anxiety and burnout. You set the tone. Your employees need to know that they do not need to absorb abuse from parents or colleagues and that you will support them. They also need to know how to constructively confront such aggression. You may need to provide training. All employees need to understand the clear expectation that they will treat fellow employees and clients with respect, even if they don't agree with them.

And when the rules are broken, there need to be individual consequences. Leaders need to confront *all* instigators.

In one study, only a quarter of targets were satisfied with the way that their organization handled the incivility they experienced. Further, the study found that other employees who witness incivility that occurs without repercussion may see such behavior as a way to get ahead (Pearson and Porath, 2005).

If there are no repercussions for the instigator, the consequences for the organization will include a loss of motivation and decreased work output. In short, you will lose your team.

No Jerk Rules for the Front Office
  Set zero-tolerance expectations.
  Train your office staff to work as a team.
  Stand up if someone leans over the desk to yell.
  Keep cool. Be polite. Be clear: bad language is not acceptable.
  Have backup in place if you have to ask someone to leave.
  When incivility occurs, act swiftly and firmly.

THINK LARGE, START SMALL.

Most of the leaders that we have known who have been successful in making positive changes in their internal communication systems have started small: a single issue or a single event. They have moved slowly, teaching their staff along the way how to respond to the new signals coming from the boss.

The important thing is that you keep talking—and listening. Be sure that your troops understand the mission and feel invested in it. Be sure they understand what you expect of them. Be sure they have the opportunity to tell you what they expect of you. Be sure they are talking to each other. Don't make assumptions. Ask.

This can be risky stuff. It may require that you throw out some old ways of thinking and leading and engage in some new habits yourself. It certainly requires that you be flexible. It requires that you are clear what *your* job is. What tasks *must* you do? What can you entrust to others? In what parts of your job can you share decision making? Are there areas of your work that you cannot or will not leave to collaboration? How comfortable are you in dealing with differences of opinion? With anger? Do you know how to build consensus? Do you need to add some skills to your toolbox? Who can teach you?

The challenge for leaders in the twenty-first century, says Wheatley, is to find ways to create the conditions that more effectively foster connections all across the organization. People to people. Go talk to the troops.

• • •

Two-way communication with your employees is fundamental to the smooth operation of your organization. Employees help make change happen. They can be a powerful marketing arm. They can provide good customer service to parents and community members. But, before they offer their help, your staff members must feel engaged in the mission of the school and the school division. Your job as leader is to make them feel part of the team.

For reflection

1. What do you know about your employees' satisfaction?
2. How can you gauge how they feel about their work?
3. How can you find out how, or if, members of the staff collaborate informally? Are their collaborations effective?
4. What three small initiatives could you begin to engage employees more in the mission of the organization? Which one might have the biggest impact?
5. What steps can you take to ensure a civil workplace?

8

NAIL YOUR SUCCESSES

Being Accountable in a Data-Driven World

Today, we make something real by assigning a number to it.

—Margaret J. Wheatley

We live in an age of accountability. Schools and school districts live and die by test scores, means, medians, averages, and bell curves. That is not all bad. When teachers and principals disaggregate (i.e., break down and analyze) scores, they gain powerful tools to help individual students learn. The department of facilities looks to the numbers to find fuel efficiencies. The human resources department examines employee retention and calculates the cost of replacing a worker. The availability of computers, spreadsheets, bar codes, and scanners has made it possible to keep better track of desks, textbooks, and travel expenses.

To maintain credibility in today's world, we must also measure the effectiveness of our communication efforts. Whether a districtwide marketing initiative or a communication component of an instructional program, it is important to know if the dollars we spend to educate our parents and community on such issues as No Child Left Behind, for instance, are being well spent. It is important to understand what works and what doesn't as we build relationships and communicate information in our own district or school building. Well-designed strategies can help us evaluate our efforts.

No matter what the project, the communication of that project needs to be an integral part of the design of the project. Measuring communication effectiveness needs to be part of the project's assessment. When a project or program is initiated without much thought being given to communication, participants are left feeling distanced from the plan and uninvolved. Yet when the same project suddenly runs into trouble, the first cry is always for "better communication."

Because midcourse corrections can prevent big and expensive mistakes, we believe that evaluation strategies that can be done relatively easily and quickly, and that give real-time feedback, are almost always winners. We recognize that school leaders find it hard to make the time to step back and take a look at what is happening. "Once the school year starts," principals and superintendents tell us, "we have no real time to breathe." We believe evaluation is not worth doing if we can't learn something, but we also believe that there is lots to learn and efficient ways of doing it.

A SHORT DETOUR INTO FAILURE

Whether in the classroom or the office, schools usually evaluate to look for what's *not* working and with an eye to quickly eliminating it. Failure, we assume, is to be avoided and erased as efficiently as possible. But, slow down a minute, could we actually learn something when things go wrong?

The corporate world struggles with the issue of failure too. Stockholders are not tolerant of expensive mistakes, but industry points with some pride to incidences where a spectacular flop has led to a subsequent triumph. It was the failure of the Edsel that led the Ford Company to conduct the research that led to the design of the enduring Mustang. Remember the scientist at 3M who created a glue that just wouldn't quite stick—and that subsequently became the Post-It Note?

Where industry has been willing to make failure an acceptable outcome and has created the mechanisms to learn from failure—rather than condemning it—business success has followed. One corporation systematically encourages the development of "popcorn stands," small, well-researched, entrepreneurial, in-house efforts that often lead nowhere, but sometimes lead the way to breakthroughs. Employee creativity thrives where duds and dead ends are not punished.

The questions that we ask when we evaluate a project or program give our staff members and our community a clue about how failure will be treated. Is there room in your organization to test an exciting new idea—even at the risk of missing the mark?

When they reflect, successful people often say that they learned far more from their failures than from their successes. There are many reasons that a project can go wrong. The idea may be a great one, but:

- It turns out to be the wrong solution to the problem.
- It has been launched without sufficient resources, either money or personnel or time.
- It has not been vetted sufficiently with the folks involved or the intended "clients" to discover what operational problems might be in store.
- The strength of the opposition to change grows much larger than anticipated.
- It is marketed to the wrong group, or not at all.

In order to do something well, we must first be willing to do it badly.

—Julia Cameron

There is a lot to learn from these slips. Some years ago, as part of a major outreach to our nonschool community, we designed a program to launch principals as speakers to community groups and organizations. We met with the principals and described the program. The superintendent publicly and enthusiastically endorsed the initiative. (Indeed, he led the way with two months of nonstop community barnstorming.) We created templates for the principals to use when speaking before the local Chambers of Commerce and citizens' associations. We published handouts to support the presentations. We gave the principals lists of contacts in their own communities so they could set up their own speaking engagements. We commissioned the principals—and waited. And waited.

As a result of all that effort, *no* principal-community contacts were ever made. Not one. The plan failed miserably. We had not tested our hypothesis with the principals carefully enough. We knew from the research that communities find principals a trusted source of school news and information. We knew from experience that our principals often spoke to their own PTA and school groups and were comfortable behind the podium. But—although the principals, when asked, said they *liked* the plan—we never asked whether individual principals would be willing to call a community organization and ask to be put on the speaker roster. It turns out, these principals weren't, and they stayed in their schools. We learned a lot from our mistake.

In general, people have a low tolerance for failure. The intense pressure in our communities for higher test scores only reinforces the perception of failure as negative. It takes skilled leadership and the kind of trust that is built over time to create a climate where bold moves that sometimes end in big pratfalls can be celebrated. But it is in that kind of climate that creativity flourishes and children learn. (Indeed, we need to teach our students the benefits of failing too.) How you evaluate your progress—even your communication efforts—will tell your employees and your stakeholders a lot about what you value.

WHO DOES THE EVALUATING?

Calling in Reinforcements

Has your district consistently had trouble passing school bonds or levies in recent years? Is the community's perception of its schools totally skewed and decidedly negative? Has there been a major breakdown in trust between school board and staff, between school and community? These are times when it may be wise to use an outside assessment team to look at the communication in your school or district. In situations like these, it can be helpful to call in an impartial outside voice to delineate the credibility gaps and offer new solutions.

A communication audit is a review of the interactions between the school or school district and all its stakeholders. It looks at such things as demographics, budgets, personnel resources, and institutional policies and practices. It also looks at local media coverage and community climate, and then analyzes how—and if—your organization's efforts are meeting community needs.

The chief advantage of an external audit is that no one has to take *your* word about the results. You have an independent voice to document where your communication efforts have worked well. If there are problems, an audit can give you clear issue definitions on which to base some new initiatives. An audit report can be the beginning of a new plan of action from which to begin to repair damaged relationships with your community.

There are a number of resources you can tap for a communication audit. The National School Public Relations Association regularly conducts communication audits in schools and school districts, using school communication professionals. A public relations or marketing firm in your community may offer such a service. Perhaps you can persuade the president of that firm (are his/her children in your schools?) to conduct an audit pro bono.

On Your Own

There are many good reasons for designing and implementing your own communication evaluation. Creating your own evaluation will probably be less costly. A home-grown process can certainly be more immediate and flexible to the needs of your program. Perhaps most importantly, it will allow you more easily to make the course corrections along the way that can be indispensable to your efforts. You won't wait six months to know why there was no change in parent opinion on the advisability of requiring school uniforms at the magnet traditional school! There are probably some excellent in-house resources available to you, should you want assistance in designing evaluation tools. Your school system's department of accountability or assessment may be helpful.

BUILDING AN EVALUATION FRAMEWORK

Whoever conducts the assessment, you and your team must think carefully about what your benchmarks should be. The old ways of measuring communication efforts almost always involved counting *output*: how many bond brochures were distributed, how many press releases got written, how many boundary information sessions or parent-teacher conferences were held. These numbers are concrete documentation that clearly track effort. They can be an important part of your overall assessment. But these numbers do not speak to the *effectiveness* of your effort. Assessing the *impact* of your communication gives you information you can use to improve.

Communication guru Pat Jackson (1994) had a mantra: Behavior, not communications or even attitudes, is the bottom line. The community must not only *think* well of their public schools, but they must also *support* the schools with their votes, their tax dollars, and their volunteer hours. They must send their children to those schools to be educated.

Whatever your project, you must use the full weight of your communication to bring about the *actions* you need to be successful. Depending on the issue, that might be a majority vote on a bond referendum, high attendance at parent meetings on the new grading system, more and better media coverage of instructional programs, or more smiles from the folks in the front office.

So how do you most easily and efficiently capture the assessment data you need?

a. *You define the problem clearly.* What's gone wrong? What do you want to be better? So many solutions miss the mark because no one clearly outlined the problem at the start. (A new newsletter won't calm the waters if what parents want is a live voice answering the phone.)

b. *You define the audience(s) you are addressing.* Good communication strategies miss the mark when they are focused on the wrong audience or no audience in particular. (You don't e-mail new research on promotion and retention to the PTA board without explanation and context.

c. *You create a careful working plan and a time frame for your efforts.* You cannot know what to assess until you decide what you are going to do.

d. *You define what success will look like.* You will need to know if people's knowledge has increased, if their attitudes have changed, and, most importantly, have they taken any *action* based on those new attitudes. You need to know not only that your messages have gotten out, but that they have been *understood*.

CHOOSING YOUR TACTICS

Some years ago, as business technology changed and improved, our school district needed to move several thousand employees from an old and beloved e-mail system to (the then new) Microsoft Office. An anticipatory wail of despair reverberated loudly throughout the district.

For months, while the technological preparations for the switch were being made, the technology and communications departments were meeting weekly, preparing and implementing a major joint communication plan to give employees information about the change and to provide a friendly face to the new software. The technological work and the communication were inextricably bound together and bound to the evaluation. We used every tactic available: information on the Web, printed information, workshops, and cameo appearances and reminders at faculty meetings. The stakes were high. Having once persuaded faculty to use e-mail (remember those days?), we now had to teach them a whole set of new skills. They were not happy.

We determined that success would mean that, in the end, teachers had to know how to use the new system (that is, that the training component worked), they had to understand the benefits of the new software program (even if they missed some of the features of the old), *and* they had to be using the new e-mail with the same—or increased—frequency with which they had used the old. Success also meant that the school system would not grind to a halt as we made the changes. We met those goals and more. Today, of course, the volume of e-mail traffic across the system stresses the (new and improved) servers and the technology team every day.

No Shortage of Tools

Once you have identified your benchmarks and you have determined what success looks like, you have only to choose the best tools. There are many available to you.

- If there are response numbers to be counted, computers can create charts and graphs that provide easy-to-grasp pictures of your progress.
- If you are communicating, at least in part, on line, tracking Web page "hits" will tell you something about your efficacy.

- Short, online surveys—created easily with today's software—can be helpful in pre- and postassessment of a project, but can also provide markers along the way. (If not all your parents have home access to the Internet, set up your computer lab on a PTA night and invite parents to tell you what they think.)
- Meeting attendance, sign-ups, volunteer hours, suggestion slips, and certainly votes can be counted.

Using Stories as Evidence

There is also a vast world of evaluative information beyond the numbers that we can gather in systematic and intentional ways. We can use the richness of our experience—as employers, as parents, as students, as neighbors and community members—to help us judge if we are moving in the right direction. How do these people feel about us or our programs? Do we have their support? Start with your project team. Debrief regularly with them about what is happening, how people view the changes, and what should happen next.

It is harder to capture a climate change in the front office than to record the number of milk cartons consumed in the cafeteria. But there are ways. Sometimes it is simply listening and documenting the stories people tell. Are you stopped often in the hallways with thanks for the new grade-reporting system? Or with horror stories about how often the new telephone system crashes? That's evaluative material. Write it down. Keep track. (The bad stories may outweigh the good ones in your head, but if you keep track on paper, you may discover otherwise.)

Sometimes, you have to seek anecdotal information in more intentional ways. After a testing irregularity caused the grades of 150 high school students to be invalidated, a principal gathered staff members to call every parent to (a) explain the situation, (b) describe the remedy (students retaking the test), and (c) gather parental feedback. It seemed like a very black moment—all those disgruntled parents. But, to his great surprise, the principal was overwhelmed with the positive response. Instead of angry tirades, the callers were thanked for the school's quick and clear response to the problem and for the effort expended to make the individual phone calls.

Small focus groups can also be an effective tool in determining whether a project is on the right track. If you have undertaken a large and long-term community campaign, checking in with stakeholders as the project proceeds to see if your messages have reached the stakeholders and, perhaps, changed some minds is a helpful thing to do. If the billboard campaign isn't working, take it down!

NO SURPRISE: IT'S ALL ABOUT RELATIONSHIPS

The ultimate test of any communication is the strength of the relationships it builds. Can you document that your relationships with your stakeholders are stronger today because of your communication efforts? Are your stakeholders more active supporters of your school or district today than they were yesterday?

When you can document what changed (or didn't), what provoked the change (or didn't), and what (if any) new actions your stakeholders have taken as a result of your efforts, you will know if you are on the right track. And all those people that you asked for help and opinions along the way now have a stake in the success of the operation.

Evaluation at its best is a continuous process. It is an inclusive process. It is often a messy process. Bottom line:

- Did you try something different?
- Did you get different results?
- Can you tell me why?

• • •

Ongoing evaluation of our communication efforts can give us critical information that helps us do our job. Evaluation of our communication efforts—whether we do the evaluating ourselves or recruit outside assistance—tells us if we are getting our messages out clearly and to the right audiences. Both statistical data and anecdotal information provide important information.

For reflection

1. What information would be helpful to have as this project proceeds?
2. What are the most efficient ways of collecting that information?
3. Who can help you gather the data?
4. What will success look like?

GET IN THE RING

Claiming Our Political Heritage

Politics is the only game for grown-ups—and too important to be left to the politicians.

—John F. Kennedy Jr.

No problem can be solved from the same consciousness that created it. We must learn to see the world anew.

—Margaret J. Wheatley

No politics in schools, you say? Puhleeezee! How would we get anything done?

Take a look at the issues that superintendents and principals grapple with every day: leading a divided school board through budgeting or redistricting, balancing factions on a PTA governing board, convincing a faculty of the benefits of reorganization, or meeting with community members to forestall an uprising over the disposal of an abandoned school building.

Webster defines *political* as "of, or relating to . . . the conduct of government . . . or concerned with the conduct of governmental policy." The dictionary defines *policy* as "a definite course or method of action selected from among alternatives and in light of given conditions to guide and determine present and future decisions." The word *govern* implies *"keeping a straight course or smooth operation for the good of the individual and the whole"* [italics added]. What is the school leader's job here but *to lead a straight course for the good of the whole*?

The bottom line is that getting things done in schools—as with any other group of people who have come together to accomplish a task—is a political act. Even if you, as principal or superintendent or department head, were able to *dictate* everything that happened in your realm, that would still be a political act. It would just mean that you were either a queen or a king.

The issues around the possession and use of power are what make people uncomfortable about "politics." Sometimes, we fear other people have more power than we do, that they will use it badly, or that we will be harmed by their "misuse" of power. Or we worry about our own ability to use power wisely and effectively. Then we abdicate power to other people and get angry when they take it. What happens in your district when a student newspaper prints a two-page spread on the life of homosexual students in the school or when the student editors level charges in the daily paper that their First Amendment rights have been curtailed? How do you respond when faculty members ask to be included in high-level discussions? These are people exercising their power.

What does power have to do with communication? Well, everything. Communication is a tool that gives you power. As we have already talked about, the use of good communication gives you the ability to lead in powerful ways. Effective communication helps you persuade people to join your team. It allows you to correctly define a problem and find a good solution. It gives you the ability to get things done *for the good of the whole*.

It is your job as leader/politician to use your words to help others see the world as you describe it. Because you are leader of a political body whose mission is to educate the community's children, your words can help create the world that you and your constituents want to build. Your responsibility as leader is to help shape and communicate a vision for your school or school system. Through your words you have the opportunity to make things better *for the good of the whole*. If you do not seize this power someone else will.

We can use communication—and, through our words, our political power—to change the way people act. This is how we get things done.

School leaders have to understand that public education is going to continue to struggle for the hearts and minds of the public. So much disinformation is out there, and some of it is intentional. Superintendents
need help telling the school district's story. It is critical to their success.
Actually it is critical to their survival.

—Dr. Curtis Culwell, Superintendent,
Garland ISD (TX) (Bagin, 2007c, p. 13)

The political goal of our communication is to create support for particular behaviors and then *cause those behaviors to happen*. This means
we first explain clearly and passionately to the community the need for
support for the school bond referendum, for instance, and then make
sure (in whatever ways are legal) that citizens get out to vote. Just creating positive public opinion does not win at the polls. You must have
the votes. Too often we make the assumption that B will follow A—and
too often we lose.

ALL POLITICS IS LOCAL—EVEN INDIVIDUAL

Politics—including school politics—does not take place in a vacuum. It
happens on the street (in the precincts, the politicians would say). You
have to know your constituents, their needs, their hopes, and their abilities. "All persons . . . want and need to be treated as distinct individuals, not just one in a crowd of followers. So, if you want to lead them,
you need to focus on and understand them as individuals" (Salacuse,
2006, p. 41). With that knowledge you begin to frame the decisions that
affect *the good of the whole*.

In *Good to Great*, Jim Collins (2001, p. 50) sets out to determine what
qualities enabled companies to achieve enduring greatness. The trans-
formation of a company begins, he found, by "getting the right people
on the bus"—that is, hiring the best you can find. "The right people will
do the right things and deliver the best results they're capable of." Your
job, as the political leader, is to find these "right people" and encourage
them to become invested in a joint enterprise. Under your leadership,
they will deliver results *for the good of the whole*.

Jazz percussionist Max Roach once told interviewer Ben Sidran that you have to shape the music you are playing around the people who are playing with you. You have to discover their strengths and use them. So it is in the best schools. The leader comes to know the people around him and, using their particular strengths, shapes the vision and the strategies they will use *for the good of the whole*.

Roach also said that you can't do again what you have already done— partly because in a new setting you are surrounded by new talent and new skills and partly because people don't want to listen to repeats. It is tempting to think, "Well, this program worked in my old school system, why not import it?" Roach would say, "Not so fast. Talk to the new people around you and start again."

TO USE POWER WISELY, YOU MUST ASK GOOD QUESTIONS AND LISTEN TO THE ANSWERS

Asking questions is a way to communicate to another person that he or she is important to you. The right questions can give you insight into his or her priorities, interests, and needs. You use those priorities to help shape your vision.

The first year that, under No Child Left Behind regulations, two Fairfax County schools were compelled to offer transfer options to parents, we worked with principals for several months in the late spring, ahead of the test score release, to prepare parents and faculty for the possibility that the school would not meet the Adequate Yearly Progress benchmarks. The school leadership explained—in publications, on the Web site, in parent meetings—why that might happen, what the changes might mean for each school, and how each school would meet the challenge.

When the scores were released, a number of parents in one of the schools requested transfer for their children. So we went back and asked them why. We learned from our surveys that—because this was a school with a high mobility rate—many families' first communication from the school was a letter in August that said the school was not making the grade. These families had only recently moved to the neighborhood and had missed all our communications in May and June.

We made the assumption that the families who were registered in June would be the same folks that would be there in September. We had not asked the right questions and did not fully understand our audience. We had missed our chance to win their support. Wrong again.

SHARING POWER BRINGS POSITIVE RESULTS

The city of Alexandria, Virginia, has only one large high school, T.C. Williams, into which all the city's students pour. Like other schools, this high school is often the battleground on which the community works out its difficulties. (The movie *Remember the Titans* is the story of the pivotal moment in Alexandria history when school desegregation played out on the T.C. football field and in its locker rooms.) The matters of this high school remain of intense interest to all parts of the community.

When it was determined that it was time to replace T.C. Williams's forty-year-old building, the superintendent and her staff built a planning initiative to include as wide a swath of citizens as possible. Community meetings were held. The faculty was asked for suggestions. Models of the proposed building were created and displayed. The school system's cable television channel carried information. Later, tours of the building-in-progress were begun.

The outreach paid off. The new facility received rave reviews—from students and staff, from parents, and from the press. The building, not originally intended to be "green," is winning national environmental awards—because a citizen in one of those early meetings was persuasive about the need to pay attention to conservation issues. The building's opening in the fall of 2007 was a cause for a huge community-wide celebration. The "green" advocate was recognized at the ribbon cutting ceremony. As a result of the community process, citizens found a renewed interest in this high school's success.

The goal is to create a climate in which you and the people you lead together make the decisions that shape the future. We once worked for a wise leader who, every time there was a decision to be made, would ask, "Who needs to be at the table?" A good question.

Bring to the table the people who will be affected, as well as the people who will implement the change. Listen to them. You will most often get better decisions, and, equally important, you will have created a group of supporters invested in seeing that the decisions that the group made are carried out. This is good use of your political power.

TO GET A GOOD DECISION, EVERYONE NEEDS THE SAME INFORMATION

Many years ago, we knew a small school division that, from the outside, seemed to be running fairly well. Inside, however, morale was low. Employees felt disenfranchised. Good programs got stalled for no apparent reason. Something was choking the system.

Months of sleuthing turned up some interesting results. All the dead ends stopped outside the door of the office of a key assistant superintendent, a well-known and respected, longtime employee who had come up through the ranks. On the surface, he seemed to be managing his duties effectively and collegially: lots of meetings involving lots of stakeholders.

In fact, he was derailing the organization by controlling information. He gave one piece of information to the first person. He gave another piece to the second person. Both pieces were accurate, but incomplete. No one, except the assistant superintendent, had enough information to make a decision alone. It left everyone else powerless.

This leader was well intentioned—he thought he had the best answers for the system and that it was quicker and easier to move ahead alone. His means were skillful—it took a long time to figure out what the problem was. But almost single-handedly he had brought the organization to a crawl.

Carville and Begala (2002, p. 97) describe it this way, "If people don't understand how their piece fits into the picture and don't understand the rationale behind the order they've been given, they're more likely to screw it up."

YOU'VE GOT TO HAVE THE STAMINA TO STAY IN THE GAME

Leadership is "about learning how to shape the future" (Jaworski, 1996, p. 3). This is a long-distance run, not a sprint.

When Major General John Stanford became superintendent of the Seattle Public Schools in September 1995, his chief liability was that he was not an educator and had never led a school system. But he knew a lot about organizations, and he knew a lot about people. His skeptics were waiting for him, but he used his assets to overcome his liability. He listened hard and reached out to build relationships quickly.

"I knew my learning curve would be steep," he wrote later. "In the opening weeks of school in Seattle, I visited several schools a day, meeting principals and talking to teachers, learning as fast as I could about the district. . . . At the same time I was visiting schools at home and around the country, I was also spending time in my new city. I was learning the neighborhoods, the culture, the politics, and the business, because I knew all of that would have an impact on the schools" (Stanford, 1999, pp. 1–2, 7).

Superintendent Stanford led the Seattle schools for only three years before he died of an unexpected and devastating illness. But in that short time, he was able to negotiate a new relationship with the teachers union, galvanize the business community to provide enormous financial support for academic programs, double the number of community volunteers in the schools, focus the whole city on the importance of reading to and with children, and, perhaps most importantly, gain the trust of Seattle's parents. He had his track shoes on.

"Love 'em and lead 'em," Stanford used to say. His love could be rapier sharp when he discovered practices that he thought were hurtful to children, but it contained huge measures of listening, relationship building, and empowering. He was a politician in the best sense of the word.

"We don't believe that brains or personality or good fortune are the most important attributes of a winner," Carville and Begala (2002, p. 19) say up front. "Perseverance. Toughness. Tenacity. *Those* are the qualities that make the difference."

Just keep going.

TO BE POWERFUL, BE A POET

"Language can reform reality." That's the assertion of poet Adrienne Rich. As a leader, you have ample opportunity to use language to make your school community a better one *for the good of the whole*. Be clear in what you say and write. As educators, we get into needless trouble by assuming that our parents understand where we are headed, just as our parents—because they once went to school—assume that they understand all about managing school.

Be curious, as poets are. Ask lots of questions. Take risks, as poets do. Test out different solutions.

Laugh together with those around you. Even in the midst of the toughest battles, humor helps to soften lines. How silly do we all look wrangling over cafeteria duty, when you take the view from 30,000 feet? Humor can be a political power tool.

And, at the risk of repeating ourselves, tell stories. More and more research confirms what the wisest leaders have always known: that the best way to communicate values, to persuade, to motivate, to lead change—that is, to do the things that politicians do—is to tell stories. We tell stories to our children without thinking about it, and we need to tell each other stories too. We get so caught up in listing our arguments that we forget that we can sometimes better convey information and commitment with our stories.

Superintendent John Stanford told a story about the day his sixth-grade teacher came to his house to inform his parents that he had failed.

> When I saw my parents' faces as they showed her to the door, I was devastated. I felt ashamed. My parents had never graduated from grade school. They each worked two jobs (my father as a truck driver and train engineer, my mother as a cook) to keep our family together and, more than anything, they wanted better for their children. . . . The jolt of letting down my family, the shame I felt as my friends moved on, the embarrassment I felt in front of my neighbors, the message my retention sent to my parents: all forced me to take my schooling, and perhaps my life, more seriously. . . . I would not be where I am today if Miss Greenstein hadn't had the courage and love to do what she did. (1999, p. xiii)

His story conveys to us, far more clearly than any exposition, the power we have as educators to make changes in children's lives. It is a pretty clear call to get going!

So, look again. Whether you are meeting with the school board, the PTA, the faculty, central office staff, or the chamber of commerce, you are in deeply mired in politics. If you were not a political animal, you would not be where you are or who you are.

Instead of trying to separate yourself from the game, claim your strength. Use the tools you have to move your school forward *for the good of the whole*. Hold the tough meetings, encourage the strategic conversations, welcome the give and take—and the tension—out of which will come better solutions for your students. Build the relationships that will support your work both inside the school and in the community. Govern well.

● ● ●

Whenever we seek to change the status quo, to make things better, we are engaging in a political act. We can choose to use power wisely or not. But not to claim our power is to forfeit the game entirely.

For reflection

1. What is your own gut response to the word *politics*?
2. Make a list of all the political acts you committed today.
3. How careful are you with your language?
4. Write a poem.
5. Did you have enough breakfast today?

10

MIND YOUR REPUTATION

Marketing Your School's (or District's) Greatness

> We all make decisions . . . as much with our hearts as with our heads.
>
> —Peter Montoya

It's a game we communication people often play. Morning coffee in hand, we scour the newspaper headlines, looking for people or organizations whose reputations have suffered a major bruising. How, we ask ourselves, would we have responded?

We gathered the following examples one random morning from the *Washington Post*, the *New York Times* and the *Alexandria Gazette*.

From the business section:

"Ford Had Its Worst Loss Ever in 2006"
"Delays Limit Robust Sales at Microsoft"
"Wal-Mart Settles U.S. Suit about Overtime"

From the education world:

"Abortion, Sexual Orientation Sample Lesson Plans Draw Discord"
"School System Resists 'No Child' Provision"
"Colleges Regroup after Voters Ban Race Preference"

From the business section:

"[Television] Anchor's Ties to Citigroup Attract Scrutiny"

That list doesn't even get us to front-page politics.

Every day, hundreds of people wake up worried about what other people are saying about them or their organizations. Corporations worry because it affects their bottom line. Not-for-profits worry because public opinion affects donations. (Think of the struggles of United Way and American Red Cross in recent years.) Politicians want to get elected. Celebrities want unbridled approbation. Community leaders want approval. We all want to be liked. Headlines like those above keep people like us employed.

WHY WORRY?

Why should a school or a school system care what people think? Why does reputation matter? Unlike our corporate brothers and sisters, we are not selling products. We do, however, depend on our communities for funding and support. When public opinion about our schools is negative, when editorials and op-ed pieces in the local press decry school policy and practice, it is harder to persuade the city council, the county board of supervisors, and the taxpayers to vote monies for new and expanding programs. The first reason schools should care is our own fiscal bottom line.

We also protect our reputation because it is the foundation on which we build relationships in the community. Everyone wants to stand next to a winner. Business partners, advocates, volunteers, political allies, mentors—the entire support network around a school or school district grows strong as the reputation of that school or system grows strong. An excellent reputation opens doors.

For years, the Economic Development Authority of Fairfax County has used the excellence of Fairfax County schools to market the economic viability of the community—both at home and abroad. If you have worked in Fairfax County Public Schools and traveled outside the state, you have often heard:

"Oh, you work for Fairfax Schools? I have heard so much about what a great system that is."

On the other hand, if you have ever worked in a system (as we have) with a poor reputation—deserved or not—you also understand the impact of reputation.

A healthy reputation allows you to lead through change. If your school or system is known as a high-quality institution, when you announce a new program or the retiring of a favorite old program, your reputation will cause your stakeholders to examine your plan in a positive, not a negative, light. When you suffer a critical incident, your reputation gives you the wiggle room you need to get through. It buys you time.

If you are doubtful about the need for a stellar reputation, remember how creative marketing changed our views about seatbelts, even before the laws were passed, about helmets for young bicycle riders, about alcohol and driving. Skilled marketing can help our customers make good decisions about their good schools.

TWO CAVEATS

You can't market a poor product. No matter how high your ratings, if you introduce a poorly conceived plan or a bad idea, it won't fly, and your reputation will suffer. No amount of marketing will help. Sooner or later, everyone recognizes lipstick on a pig.

You can't market a poorly aligned product. If you have a great plan for using the new school marquee, but what your parents need is more timely information on your website, you lose. Before you go public with any initiative, you must be sure that it is the right one in the right place at the right time. Building your reputation successfully requires that you are also careful about how you use it. Your reputation rests on excellence, integrity, and trust.

IF YOU DON'T MANAGE YOUR
REPUTATION, SOMEONE ELSE WILL

School leaders shy away from the word *marketing*. It sounds commercial. In fact, marketing is simply a matter of minding your own reputation. Nature abhors a vacuum. If you don't spread the good word about what you are doing well, someone will fill the air with bad words about your shortcomings. If you are proud of what is happening in your schools—and, in general, we school people are—then it should not be a hard job to say so. Marketing, like other forms of communication, requires attention and thought. It is an intentional process.

As a local council election was heating up, it became apparent to the superintendent that the school system might well become the center of negative attention from candidates on all sides—not because it was a failing system, but because there was a dearth of other "sexy" topics for debate in the community that year. The superintendent launched his own marketing campaign. He endorsed no candidates, but went on the stump through the community, spreading the good news about the system—rising test scores, successful new programs, and student academic prowess. He visited every council candidate and provided information about the school system, inviting each candidate to visit his or her local school. At the end of the campaign, every council candidate was on record praising the accomplishments of the school system. Every candidate claimed, at least in part, to be responsible for the schools' good record.

That superintendent was able to move in a proactive and preventive way, but sometimes you don't see the arrow coming until it hits. Don't let unwarranted public attacks on your school or school system stand unanswered. The temptation is to ignore the strikes and not to make a second-day story. That almost always turns out to be a mistake. Silence may encourage more attacks, and it almost always demoralizes employees and supporters who feel the sting as much as you do.

MARKETING IS EVERYBODY'S RESPONSIBILITY

Most days, most schools and school systems neither receive a national award nor suffer a major bomb threat. Reputations thus are made or broken on smaller things, like how quickly and cooperatively solutions are found, how accessible the boss and her staff are, how accurately snow days are called.

Reputations are also made on the backs of what industry calls "tangibles," that is, the appearance of things such as the cleanliness and brightness of the school, the appropriateness of staff members' dress, the clarity and accuracy of printed material and the website, the hospitality with which visitors are greeted, even the placement of visitor parking spaces. These are all visible clues to employees and guests alike that this school or system is a place of respect, a place where people take care of each other and their work (Zeithaml, 1996, pp. 118, 120, 122, 306). Stakeholders' trust is built in tiny increments. The fact that the sidewalks are well shoveled no matter how much snow falls, and that the halls are shiny clean every day builds reputation.

Tending to all these small details is the job of everyone in the organization. The boss doesn't do this alone. The boss's job is to set the tone and lead the way. As management guru Tom Peters used to say, you must pay attention to the people who can move the ball down the field. In the case of marketing, that includes bus drivers, food services workers, front-office staff, and groundskeepers, among others.

BUILDING YOUR MARKETING PLAN

Marketing builds strong relationships with employees, parents, and neighbors and protects your reputation in the community. It provides information to your stakeholders and moves them to action.

We are all about plans that work, not beautiful notebooks on the office shelf. Stick to the basics. You can start small. The community is primarily interested in three things about schools: Are they safe? Are the kids learning? Are we getting good return on our tax dollar? Parents today add another question: How am I included in the process? A marketing plan built around one or more of these questions is a winner.

You may need to focus your efforts on a particular issue. Do you need to tout the school system's academic strength? Do you need to broadcast the changes in your special education services? Do you want to be known as a friendly and welcoming place? A good place to work?

Americans are much more conscious about what they eat and what their children eat than they used to be. It's a hot topic these days—one that the news media loves to talk about, particularly if it appears that student interests are not being well served. School nutritionists and food service workers are constantly fielding requests from families that eat a vegan or vegetarian diet; parents of students with food allergies; and citizens with other concerns about obesity, school menus, or food preparation.

As parent demands began to grow, one school district undertook a well-orchestrated but quiet campaign about its food. When the district opened its doors to a health department inspection, it also agreed to welcome the television news cameras that wanted to tag along. The public relations office began sending food story briefs in its regular Friday e-mail to media. These included nutritional information about school lunches, a description of the taste-testing events held for student food tasters who help to choose cafeteria items, and media releases on all the awards the department won. The food service director gave interviews. Over time, the campaign created the backdrop against which other food stories were written. The department became known as "the award-winning food services department," even when under public attack from outside watchdog groups.

Such "marketing" initiatives don't have to be focused just on members of the press. They can be focused on parents ("The school system is now offering college and financial aid counseling for students and their families, and here is how you can avail yourselves of them"), on employees ("You will now be able to access your benefit information on line and, annually, make changes to your benefit structure. Here's how") or on the community ("October is open house month at Ruffner High School! Come see a play, hear a concert, or sit in on an English class").

Your goal is to build relationships. Effective marketing provides specific information about a particular topic, but good marketing also tells a story. It appeals to the emotion as well as to the intellect. Over time, focused marketing can move a specific group of people to very specific action, though the benefits of marketing may not necessarily show up immediately. Marketing has a timed-release effect. That is what distinguishes it from crisis management. Marketing is about the long haul.

Branding can:

- Capture the imagination and help consumers make an emotional connection
- Reflect in an image or a phrase the organization's culture and values
- Build credibility
- Communicate simply and effectively through design consistency
- Claim a key position in the consumer's mind

(Carr, 2007)

IS BRANDING RIGHT FOR YOU?

"Branding" has become a marketing buzzword. A brand is a kind of shortcut that, in one image or phrase, conveys to the consumer a positive value about your school or school district. A brand is a promise made to stakeholders.

Effective brands are hard to come by. (The GEICO gecko did not just show up on the boss's desk with coffee one bright morning.) Unfortunately, in schools, branding often means slapping an ill-conceived slogan and logo on all publications. In some school systems every department and program has its own logo, leaving the public confronted with a confusing array of visual images that end up signifying little. The promise of the brand is not always kept.

Good branding is built on the same principles as all good marketing. Only when a brand is the product of thoughtful consideration, planning, and skillful design can it make a difference.

Branding Should Reflect Answers to These Questions

- What makes your school or district different or unique?
- What can your school or district truly own in the marketplace?
- What does your school or district do better or more than everyone else?
- What one benefit or message is the most compelling?
- What will connect emotionally the most with your target audiences?
- What reasons can we develop to support our claim?

(Carr, 2007)

GOOD MARKETING MANAGEMENT

Marketing is not rocket science. The important components of a marketing plan are little different than the components of any good project plan.

You will need to define clearly the issue you are addressing and your audiences. It may be the whole community, but it could be a much smaller segment of your audience. Be sure to assess the risks of your effort and identify the people in the community who can serve as your sponsors and key communicators. Figure out what tactics you will use and how you will know that you have succeeded.

Once you have organized your plan, one good way to test it out is with an elevator speech. You and I meet in an elevator in the central office building. In the time it takes for us to travel from the parking garage below to the superintendent's office on the fifth floor, can you clearly define your marketing initiative, its mission and overall strategy, and why I should help?

MARKETING TACTICS THAT WORK

There are many tactics to choose from. The caution is that the ones that you love most may not fit in every situation. Often, the best tactics are extensions of the ones you have in place already—the tools that you already use to spread the word, like faculty meetings or parent coffees. That energy just needs to be repurposed, and the messages reshaped. Tactics don't have to be big and hairy. Small steps often work better. The most important parts of marketing are the intention, the focus, and the planning.

Whatever your plans, be sure that your employees are first on the information and marketing lists. Employees are your most important stakeholders. They are always the key to success.

Parents, particularly parents of elementary children, like hands-on tactics. They like to hear about their own children. They like to see and touch the products. Younger parents like lots of information, preferably on the Web where they can access it from work and at odd hours of the day and night. Backpack letters work in the younger grades, but (do we need to say this?) hardly ever work in high school. E-mail—carefully used in connected communities—is great. In schools, events that include food are most always deemed a success. Babysitting for younger siblings is a good way to get folks out to hear your message.

The media can be an important part of your plan, but it shouldn't be the first thing you think of. You control the information that goes on your website and in your e-mails and calls. You don't control what is reported on the evening news. That said, including reporters is always better than keeping them out. Invite them to tea. Take them on a tour of the school. Tell them about your new programs and initiatives and why they are important. If you can help them figure out a timely lead, maybe they will write that good news story you've been hoping for.

Don't forget about elected officials and other key leaders in your community. Having them involved on the front end of your initiative is better than having them attack on the back end. If you can't get them to visit you, go visit them. Take them information and leave an open-ended invitation to visit.

MARKETING AND LEADERSHIP

When all is said and done, the only thing in this life you can truly claim is your reputation. That is true of your personal reputation and of the reputation of the organization you lead. You should never take it for granted. Its value is beyond measure. It is well worth your time and effort to protect.

A worn and yellowing sign hangs over the desk of a businessman in our neighborhood. He is a graduate of a local high school and once a world-class amateur athlete. The sign says:

"Do what you've always done, and you will get what you have always gotten."

In the old days, when we launched an initiative, asked for more funding, or changed our staffing formulas, the community nodded its agreement. Life is more complicated now, and we must make our case clearly and often to whoever will listen. What we "always got" is no longer enough. That is what marketing is all about.

• • •

Protecting and enhancing the reputation of your school or school district should be a priority for all school leaders. If you don't take charge, someone else will. Marketing—getting clear, timely, and compelling information to your stakeholders—needs to be carefully planned and executed. Its chief aim is to build fruitful relationships between your school or district and the community.

For reflection

1. What marketing initiative could benefit your school or school division?
2. Sketch out a possible plan:
   a. Goal
   b. Theme
   c. Audience
   d. Tactics
3. Who would you put on your marketing team?

III

THE SPECIAL INTERESTS

INVEST IN THE MEDIA

Protecting Your Assets

Others go to where the puck is. I go to where the puck will be.

—Wayne Gretsky

If you don't return my phone call, you can't influence my story.

—Jay Mathews, *Washington Post* reporter

Schools need to change the way they do business with the media. New technologies are changing how information spreads in our world. The media itself is changing, and our old attitudes of "not really your business" won't work any more. The old "No comment" and "We really can't talk about that" stance that school leaders used to employ has little meaning when cell phone videos, social media, and the Internet spread a story no matter what we do or don't say. When a reporter calls your office to tell you that he is talking by cell phone to a student in one of your high school classrooms who is reporting that a teacher has struck a student with a chair, you can no longer say, "I'm quite sure that would never happen."

YOU MUST BUILD RELATIONSHIPS

At lunch recently, a beat reporter who covers local school news told us, "We get calls from parents everyday. Sometimes we get flooded with calls. It's always an angry parent who wants us to write about his or her particular issue or injury. That's why it is *so* important for superintendents and principals to build relationships with reporters. We need to know who you are. We need to be able to talk with you. Otherwise, we hear only one side of the story."

"You may not let me into your building, but I am already in your school," *Washington Post* education reporter Jay Mathews tells principals. "All I have to do is stand across the street when school dismisses, and I can find out what is going on." But, as he points out, what he learns on the street corner is, indeed, only one side of the story. School leaders need to make their side heard too.

Good relationships with reporters are not created overnight. It takes careful, thoughtful, sometimes time-consuming, work on your part. But find a way, because when the chips are down—whether it is a tornado touching down or the day that the kindergarten student gets left on the bus—your return on your media investment will be substantial.

- Invite a reporter and his or her editor to an on-the-record discussion of the new curriculum *before* it appears in the classroom.
- Host a press open house to show off the new school renovations *before* the school reopens.
- Hold an annual press conference to introduce reporters to the superintendent's new budget, *before* it is publicly presented.
- Allow a seasoned reporter to spend time in your school to write a story about a unique teacher, the thriving drama program, or the difficulties encountered by students who do not speak English as a native language.
- When a hot education topic hits the national news, figure out a related story in your district that might interest a local reporter. (If you want to know what's "hot," Mathews says, read *Education Week*. All the best editors and education reporters take their lead from its front page.)

"A school leader has to be able to translate what is going on inside a school or school system to the people on the outside," the reporter told us at lunch. "It's complicated, and the leader has to make the time and effort to help us understand."

While editors and publishers may be worried about sales and market shares, reporters see their job as one of helping the community figure out what is taking place in schools. School people, on the other hand, continue to make the assumption that everyone understands education and that reporters' motives are suspect. We need to get beyond our blind spots and become first-class interpreters for the media in our community.

Having a good relationship with a reporter or editor also means that you can call that reporter when a story goes bad. If you feel that the reporter has been unfair, you can say so. You can ask: "What didn't you understand?" You can say: "I felt you misrepresented the school's point of view." And, if it is true, you can certainly say, "I was misquoted." Don't yell or threaten. Be clear about the error you see.

Such a conversation is more likely to have an impact if you and the newspaper or television station have a sturdy, ongoing relationship. You may get a correction or even a new story. At the very least, you will glean information from the conversation that will help you the next time.

Print reporters and their news editors do not write headlines. Headline editors or copy editors do. Television reporters do not write the often inflammatory story "teases" that appear before the commercial break. Be careful to distinguish which words in the story are incorrect or unfair. Be careful where you lay blame.

Perhaps the most important relationship you can build in the media arena is with your district's public information officer (PIO) or communications team. Every school district funnels media calls differently. In some districts all media calls go through the public information office. In others, the media are welcome to call the superintendent, principals, or department heads directly. However it works in your system, all media communication needs to be coordinated. Nothing builds suspicion and distrust faster than conflicting stories coming from inside the organization.

School communications officers have practice and expertise in working with reporters and balancing the needs of the press with those of students and school leaders.

From their office, they can see the big picture. They

- Have the time to build relationships with reporters.
- Track which reporters are following which stories.
- Are aware of media trends and groundswells (as in, "This month's flavor is 'what are schools doing for students with autism'").
- Take the pulse of the community to discover the stories that need to be told.

Call on your communication team. They can help you with talking points, coach you through an interview, and back you up when you say "no."

GROUND RULES FOR SCHOOL LEADERS

Principals and superintendents we've known tend to be far too wary of reporters. Yes, you can get a bad story. And, yes, we have all run into a reporter or editor with an axe to grind. But, bottom line, if you don't get into the game, there is no chance of winning. If you don't talk to reporters, you never have the chance to frame the story with your facts and your wisdom. You never have the chance to make your case.

In relationships with reporters and editors, there are a few, simple guidelines that all school leaders should follow:

- Be available. Sometimes easier said than done, but schools and school systems miss too many opportunities for good press by putting reporters off. An elementary principal we know launched a year-round school program that quickly became hugely popular. When it was time for new families to sign up for the next year, a line of parents formed outside the school on a cold, rainy Sunday in March, prepared to camp out the night to be sure their children got on the list. A local reporter got a tip and, wanting to do a Monday story on this school success, called the principal that Sunday afternoon for an interview. The principal was watching a ball game and refused to talk with the reporter because it was Sunday. The story never ran!

- Be honest. If we want the media to carry our good news stories, we have to ground our media relationships with honesty about problems that need to be addressed. The more candid we are about these issues the more apt we are to get the coverage we want on the good days. "Eventually, the truth comes out." Our reporter smiled at us over her sandwich. "Trying to cover up only damages the relationship. Better to just say 'We made a mistake.'"
- Repeat your vision, over and over. Frame all your conversations with reporters—whatever the topic—in the context of your larger vision for the school and the school system. Keep the vision student centered. Include the community (and the media, as the community's champion) as a partner in supporting that vision.

Reporters are human. Reporters have a job to do. A lot of them on the school beat are very young. Many of the ones who show up don't know a lot about education, but they have to get a story for their editor. They have deadlines. They have a lot less job security than we do. Reporters appreciate any help they can get. It is hard to write a totally negative story about a person who has given you access to the information you need. Build relationships.

Ask reporters what their deadlines are and try to be accommodating.

- To make the five or six o'clock news, TV reporters generally need to finish their story by midafternoon.
- Talk radio goes live 24/7.
- A reporter from a daily paper usually has until 5 or 6 p.m. to file a story for the following day.
- The weekly reporter's deadline depends on what day of the week the paper goes to bed.

GROUND RULES FOR REPORTERS

While the reporter may be asking the questions, you have not lost your advantage. You are meeting on *your* turf, your office or school grounds. The topic is one about which *you* know the most: *your* school or school district. Even if the day has been full of surprises—who suspected that your attendance clerk had been financing her house renovations with school funds?—*you* are the one who knows best about what steps are being taken to remedy the situation.

You can set ground rules about the time and place of your meeting, about the issues to be discussed, about where cameras can and can't go on school property, about what documents that can be shared. For any number of legitimate reasons—legal, personnel, student privacy—there are times when you cannot disclose everything you know. Say so. Be as candid as you can about as much as you can, and when you cannot, explain why.

What makes reporters bristle is the perception of arbitrary stonewalling. The words "No comment" should never come out of your mouth. Those words signal that you know the answer and are keeping it a secret. You are much better served by taking the long way around: "We don't know the answer to that question yet. We are currently talking with everyone involved in the incident. When we have answers, we will call you." (Then, of course, you have to do what you have promised!)

GIVING AN INTERVIEW

When you meet any reporter, be prepared. Give accurate information. If you don't know the answer, say so. If you can get the answer later, assure the reporter you will do that, and when. As tempting as it might be, never speculate about what did happen or about what might happen. Stay on the record. Going off the record can be dangerous. Don't say *anything* you wouldn't want to see on the front page tomorrow.

At the beginning of any interview, set clear expectations with the reporter about what you can talk about. If you are discussing a police incident, send the reporters to the police for details of the investigation. That is not your territory. If it is a health issue, send the reporters to the public health office or the hospital. What you can legitimately talk about is the fact that an event took place at your school or school system, that you are working closely with public safety or public health officials, and that you and other school officials are taking steps to ensure the safety and welfare of the students and staff members.

Providing reporters with a short list of steps that parents can take with or for their children relative to the incident can be helpful. (For instance, "Talk to your children about not getting into cars with strangers.") Get the reporter who is interviewing you engaged in helping you help parents and kids. It gives them a positive angle for their story.

What do you want to say? Before you do an interview, take time—even if it is only a couple of minutes—to decide on the three most important points *you* want to make. This interview gives you the opportunity to say what *you* want to say, no matter what the reporter's questions. Write your messages down if that helps.

If the issue is a bus accident, your messages might go something like:

- The children are safe.
- We are working with the police to discover what really did happen.
- Tomorrow, when the children come back to school, we will. . . .

If the issue is test scores, you might say:

- Here is where our students shine:
- The scores reaffirm these areas that need improvement:
- This is what we are doing about it:

No matter what questions you are asked, be sure that you make *your* points. It's okay, and often highly advisable, to keep repeating these answers. In fact, in a tough interview, where the reporter keeps asking the same question in different ways, the more your answers remain clear and consistent, the fewer ways the reporter has to chip away at your story. ("As I have already said, the key point is that all the children are safe. They evacuated the bus quickly and quietly and no one was injured.")

At the beginning of any interview, introduce yourself to the reporter and the camera person, if there is one, and ask what information they are looking for so that you can order your thoughts. You may also carefully suggest to them questions that you think are important. ("You

might want to ask me about the bus driver's superlative driving record.")
It offers the reporter information she may not have and the opportunity
for a better interview. That makes it a win-win affair.

Prepare fact sheets, key points, and timelines. Supposing the issue is
introducing a new math textbook and a segment of your community remains skeptical about the choice of publishers. Do you have a couple of
key, well-respected education reporters in town? Invite them for lunch,
show them the books, and offer them some fact sheets about the new
plan and how it will be implemented. Take the time to answer their
questions carefully. Court their interest. And be sure to offer the same
courtesy to your student newspaper editors.

Have a simple, up-to-date, one-page fact sheet about your school or
school district always available (number of students, number of faculty
and staff, faculty degrees, special programs, contact information, etc.).
Use it for media, new parents, and community visitors.

Manage, through your reporters, the community's expectations of
what this plan will and won't do or how this issue can, or cannot, be resolved. Reporters, too, make assumptions about your schools, your resources, and your ability to get things done. It is important to point out
budget and personnel restraints, unwieldy community expectations, and
time limitations.

Stay ahead of the game. Figure out what the reporters and the community will want to know. That may not be exactly the same as what you
would like to say. You may be extremely proud of how hard you worked
to squeeze tight resources to reallocate all the art, music and P.E. teachers on a more equitable schedule. What your parents want to hear is
how much of each of those subjects their children will receive every
week. That's the headline. Your sweat equity (no matter how brilliant)
won't interest anyone.

Paint pictures, tell stories. Use comparisons:

- "The number of students in Fairfax County Public Schools is equal
  to the size of many towns in Virginia. In our cafeterias we are feeding a small city every day."

- "Our school is back to normal. I walked the halls this morning, and students are in their classrooms, intent on their work. I watched our art students finishing up the new mural in the gym."

Stories have tremendous power to communicate what declarative sentences and numbers leave bare.

Let your body speak for you. Be friendly. Smile. Speak slowly and clearly. Keep steady eye contact. Gesture. Shake hands. In his celebrated communication study, Dr. Albert Mehrabian at UCLA (1981), determined that 38 percent of your message is delivered by the sound of your voice, 55 percent of your message in nonverbal ways, and only 7 percent by your words!

It is definitely important to have the message right. It is equally important that you project a calm and confident manner and convey that you are taking good care of the community's children. Your audience takes its cue from how you look, not what you say.

Maintain control of what comes out of your mouth. If you do not use heavily loaded words, you cannot be quoted in print or edited on television talking about "scandal" or "chaos." Never repeat or accept negative assumptions:

Reporter's question: "How are you going to deal with this *tragedy*?"

Your answer: "What we need to focus on here is that the children are all safe."

If you expect some really tough questions, stage a mock interview before the reporter arrives. Get someone to ask you about the hard issues and smooth out your answers. Breathe slowly and deeply. Literally, practice keeping your heart rate down.

You can also ask that person to sit with you in the interview, preferably behind the interviewer, so you can watch his or her face for danger cues. There are many things to focus on during an interview, and an observer may catch something you miss. (A telephone interview can be easier, if you can negotiate it. You can take notes while the reporter is talking, and you can also have your own, previously prepared, notes in front of you.)

Craft your exit line. Being able to get out of an interview gracefully is another way to set boundaries. It can be as simple as "Thank you very much for coming." Or "When we have more information, we will contact you." Or "I have a 2 p.m. meeting now, and must leave you." The point is that if you know how (and when) to leave, you remain in control of the interview. The emphasis is on the *graceful* exit.

It is never over until the reporter leaves the property. Most reporters play fair. They need you to trust them too. They want to be able to call again. Occasionally, however, a reporter steps over the line. One reporter came to interview an elementary principal in her office. After the conversation, the principal engaged the reporter in friendly conversation while walking him back to his car at the edge of the campus. After saying good-bye, the principal turned her attention to the student dismissal in progress behind her and began to direct students to their buses. She missed the fact that the reporter did not get into his car, but rather made his way back through the mass of students and teachers into the building. He found a teacher on the second floor hall, told her that he had just been with the principal who had given her permission for the teacher to talk with him. The teacher spoke truthfully about her own experience, but it was only a part of the story. Unfortunately, her view shaped the entire story.

No issue is too small to handle well. Not long ago, a student called a local talk radio station to complain that his high school had no toilet paper in the bathrooms. The station called the school, and an associate principal confirmed that, in fact, the school system often ran out of supplies like soap and toilet paper. Within an hour it was on the news wires across the country that one of the largest and finest school systems in the country had budgeted so poorly that, even though it was only November, they had run out of bathroom supplies.

The truth, when we got to the bottom, was that the school-based person in charge of ordering supplies from the central warehouse hated her job, and the school often went days without toilet paper because she neglected to order enough from the central supply warehouse. The employee issue clearly needed to be addressed, but not by the Associated Press.

The sooner you tell the bad news—and the more detail you use—the better. The roof of an elementary school caved in one night under extraordinarily heavy snow and ice. The next day, the school system quickly issued media releases with as much detail about the incident as possible. The principal set the PTA telephone tree in motion. As soon as the building was declared structurally secure, we held a press conference and took media cameras on tours of the affected area. We put out as much bad news as we could find: the extent of the damage, an early cost estimate, and the delay of school classes. With that behind us—on the second day—the news stories turned almost immediately to the school's efforts to rebuild and the spirit of cooperation in the neighborhood. Parents stopped by the trailer where the crisis response team was working, bringing coffee and donuts to thank us for getting out the word to them so quickly. Despite the cost of the repairs and the loss of instructional time, this became a good news story!

Reporters and television cameras are not the only avenues through which information flows to the community today, but they still play a key role in painting a picture of the school division and its employees. We and the media share a goal of creating an educated community. We all believe that our society is built on an informed public that is able to make good decisions. If we are at odds at times on particular issues, we must always remember what we have in common.

Media folks are worth your attention. By building solid, open, honest relationships with the reporters who show up on your doorstep, you give yourself the best chance of a fair and honest story—no matter what the breaking news.

• • •

Building good relationships with members of the media in your community can bring fair and accurate coverage about your school or district. Understanding a few rules of the game and always treating reporters and editors with respect will earn their respect of you. Clarity, consistency, and courtesy count.

For reflection

1. Which media outlets in your community (newspapers, radio, television) carry the weight of public opinion?
2. Do you know the reporters who work for these papers and stations?
3. What steps could you take to build stronger relationships with these reporters and their editors?
4. What features or events or people or programs at your school or district are the most likely to capture the attention of local citizens?
5. What is unusual or special about your school or district?
6. Could you build reporter contact into my regular schedule?

12

LEAD THE CHANGE

Modeling a Compelling Message on Diversity

Insight, I believe, refers to the depth of understanding that comes by setting experiences, yours and mine, familiar and exotic, new and old, side by side, learning by letting them speak to one another.

—Mary Catherine Bateson

In Fairfax County, the change happened very quickly. In little more than twenty years, the once bucolic district with its horse farms and largely white population became a sprawling, urban landscape of shopping centers, traffic jams, and discrete communities of immigrants from all across the world. As has happened in other communities-in-transition, the schools in Fairfax County were among the places where these changes could first be seen.

- In 1985, 80 percent of the students were white. In 2005, the percentage dropped to 50.
- The number of students in English as a Second Language classes more than doubled in those years.
- The county remained one of the richest in the country, but suddenly the number of school children who receive free or reduced-priced meals reached 20 percent.

Classrooms no longer looked as they once had. They became rainbow-colored, and all the issues of living in a diverse world were sitting squarely before school leaders.

Embracing change is not easy—either for individuals or for organizations. And meeting the challenges of community-in-transition calls for big changes, including changes in how the school division communicates with its families. It would be nice to say that translating the school newsletter into several languages, engaging one or more interpreters for PTA meetings, and holding an annual international night potluck dinner would do the trick. These gestures are important first steps to symbolize a school's commitment to embracing diversity. But they are only the beginning. The challenge is much bigger than that.

Telling Your Story

The order in which you give people information matters. Say you have three components of a compelling message about your school's diversity: individual stories of student success, facts and figures about your diverse school environment, testimonials from community members about the value of diversity. Telling them in this order creates a more compelling message than if you were to do so in reverse order. Why? Starting with a story shows rather than tells, accesses your audiences emotional brain and lets them experience the message you're sending.

MEET THE CHALLENGE

Bailey's Elementary School in Fairfax County is a school that has met the challenge of a growing diversity head-on. Bailey's largest student group is Hispanic (48 percent). The rest of the membership is divided among white (26 percent), Asian (14 percent), black (6 percent), and other (6 percent) students. Fifty-four percent of the students receive free or reduced-price meals. Forty-five percent are designated as Limited English Proficient. Not only is there ethnic and economic diversity at Baileys, but also their students practice many faiths. Religious holidays come all year long. Religious customs require students to eat different foods and sometimes to fast, to wear—or not wear—certain dress, and to pray regularly at different times of day.

Years ago, Bailey's faculty and staff determined that to be effective in educating their community's children, they could not be perceived as being at odds with their constituent families. The school needed to position itself at the center of the community, not at one end of a tug of war. It needed to be a place where all parts of the community could come together with trust to solve the problems and issues that arose from all the differences. When there is a problem in the community now, the leadership of all the faiths unites with the school to craft a solution.

School leaders address infrastructure needs to make the process work. Here are some practices:

- A determined effort to match staff ethnic demographics with those of students. Staff heritage is showcased and honored.
- A front-office staff with members who have second-language skills.
- A parent liaison, who has transformed her office into a comfortable meeting place for parents. Her work develops strong partnerships with local nonprofits.
- A series of workshops for new staff members to help them understand the impact of culture on learning and coach them on the school's collaborative culture, one that embraces cultural heritage.

ESTABLISH A STRONG FOUNDATION

So how do you make this kind of change happen? First, you must build a base of support. The smart school leader brings community representatives together. The school district does not exist in isolation, nor should it act apart from the community. Those outside the school walls must be included as part of a team that names the issue and embraces solutions. Community leader support—especially in developing citizen consensus—is essential.

The committee's initial charge should be a discussion that results in a public awareness campaign. All citizens need information—facts and figures—as well as a compelling vision for a community's future. Both of these tools—information and vision—go a long way toward moving the public forward.

There is another vital component to creating a community that thrives on its diversity—that is leadership. Even though change often starts at the grass roots of an organization, it can be created and maintained effectively solely at the grass roots for only a limited time. True systemic change throughout a school or school system requires a clear voice at the top saying "this is what we will do, and we will begin now." At some point, the leader must declare the mission in very public and very positive ways. Resources must follow. It is important that a clear message be sent to the stakeholders, both inside and outside the organization.

In any organization, 15 percent of the folks will embrace a well-presented, new idea immediately. These are the early adopters. (They were, bless them, the first to carry PDAs and cell phones.) Another 15 percent of the folks will *never* think that the idea has merit. It is with the 70 percent of the group in the middle—who initially remain undecided—that a leader must exert his energy. These are the folks who must come to understand why the new idea is important and how it will positively affect their lives. The superintendent carries those messages for the district; the principal carries them for the school. Without that leadership, eventually, the front line will sag under the weight of the job.

It's very tempting to ignore this work. One high school community we know operated with blinders, believing that if they focused on the rich white kids they could overshadow the diversity that was on their doorstep. Leaders were afraid to raise the issue, being seduced by a new school building and an active white parent community. The disaffection didn't come immediately, but as years went by and diversity increased, the issue became the elephant in the room. The whispers turned into active chatter on the community grapevine. Eventually white parents voted with their feet, enrolled their children in private schools or circumvented the system to "pupil place" them at another division school. Today, the school is underenrolled, facing a community crisis that involves boundary changes. It didn't have to be that way.

Another school district took a different approach. New state legislation mandated that minority students from a nearby city be bused to their small town high school. The superintendent saw this as an opportunity to bring the community together to embrace its newest students. She brought in leaders from the business, religious, and parent communities to form a committee that would develop strategies to make the new students welcome and help them be successful. They created messages and informed the community in newspapers, from pulpits, and at meetings. The committee continued to meet periodically once the school year was underway.

Into the second year of the program, a racial incident occurred. (Yes, it happens even when you are doing the right things.) But the superintendent called together her committee. They worked on solutions and messages and put out information. Together, they addressed the issue. The strong base of support turned what could have been a flashpoint into a moment that showcased community work at its best.

TEACH THE ADULTS

"My teachers don't want to change. They say it's too much work. They say that these newly arrived parents need to learn to do things *our* way."

Learning to accommodate—and even enjoy—the changes presented to us because we live in an increasingly diverse society is difficult, particularly because we are meeting people who do not look like we do, dress or eat as we do. We speak different languages, call our God by different names, and even practice a different code of social manners. These differences produce visceral responses in each of us that we are not always aware of and certainly don't always understand. This is not like changing the procedures for marching to and from a school assembly. Diversity challenges us in our gut.

Michael Fullan (2001) describe culture change as one with a nonlinear environment, with no easy checklist for success, but great potential for creative breakthroughs. Don't expect the change to be without accompanying messiness.·

One way to soften the emotional blow is to provide classroom teachers with lots of very practical technical assistance. Change the habits first; the emotions will follow. Sylvia Link, manager of communications services in the Peel District schools in Ontario, Canada, told us:

Teachers want to do well. They are afraid of making mistakes. We have found that providing the teachers with lots of materials on how to encourage respect and cooperation that can be used in the classroom and with parents helps a lot. It makes teachers feel secure. It gives them confidence.

We also use peer communication as a way to support the changes. Teachers helping teachers. And we engage the students and parents in telling teachers that they are doing a good job.

Arlington County (Virginia) continues to put diversity on the front burner of staff development. Several years ago, the school division conducted an audit to measure its cultural competence. Results of the audit were used to pinpoint issues and to direct solutions. A cultural competence advisory board was formed with employees representing all parts of the system. The school system's strategic plan emphasizes diversity in its value statements and student achievement goals.

Acknowledging that honest conversations are crucial to effectiveness in addressing the issue, Arlington leaders developed a framework for stakeholders to talk, listen, and learn from each other. Employee and parent groups talk with each about race and its impact on student achievement.

From meaningful dialog, solutions emerge. It takes time and patience. It takes intention and persistence. Wholesale change, especially in issues as long-standing and deep-seated as issues of race and diversity, doesn't happen overnight. Small changes, though, do happen. Be on the look out for them; hold on, acknowledge, and publicize them. They will be the ones that get the flywheel of change moving.

Keep the Conversation Going

Raising the issue of diversity is only the first step. A successful leader turns the issue into a vibrant long-term conversation complete with updates and stories of what's working and what's still challenging. Commitment to the issue includes inspiring your audience to keep talking and motivating yourself to keep listening.

DIVERSITY IS ABOUT EVERYONE

One of the most important messages that the leader must carry is that embracing life in a diverse community enriches *everyone*. It's *not* just about being hospitable and helping poor people who can't read the language or who worship in strange ways. *Everyone* learns and grows in the process.

Author Eileen Kugler (2002), whose two children attended a public high school with a richly diverse student body, used their rich experience as a springboard to champion the value that diversity brings to a school.

"Not only must our students learn how to function in a diverse global marketplace," Kugler writes, "they must be educated participants in our global society" (xxii).

Alexandria, Virginia, is a city in the greater Washington, D.C., metropolitan region. Its sole high school, T.C. Williams, is a working example of the richness that diversity offers students and the community. T.C. has gained recognition in recent years because of the movie *Remember the Titans*, about its football team that won the state championship as the school district was struggling with integration. That was forty years ago. Now, Alexandria's black and white students have been joined by students from all over the world. Its student membership currently is African American, 43 percent; Asian-Pacific, 7 percent; Hispanic, 25 percent; Native American, .2 percent; and Caucasian, 24 percent.

With some regularity, T.C. teachers bring back alumni currently in college to talk to the high school students about postsecondary education. Invariably, the conversation turns at some point to what in their high school experience turned out to be valuable in college. One skill that all the alums mention is the ability to get along with all types of people. "So many kids who went to high school only with kids like themselves just don't know how to relate in the big world." It is a source of pride among T.C. Williams's graduates.

WHAT DOES SUCCESS LOOK LIKE?

So what might a school that successfully embraces students from many countries, cultures, languages, and religions look like? The first answer is that it looks like any other friendly, welcoming school, except perhaps that it is more colorful, its sounds are more varied, and its fabric, richer.

It is most likely a school where there are documents and bulletin boards in many languages. There may be a parent liaison working in the front office. There may be an area equipped with toddler toys, full of toddlers and mothers nearby. There may be a room, with a staff member, dedicated as a "parent education center." There may be a room where students can go to pray undisturbed during the day. Somewhere, there will be available written policies (either of the school system or at least of the school) that declare a belief that people of differing cultures and faiths can come together around shared goals and that delineate practices that encourage respect and understanding.

This is probably a school where the principal can be seen often in the halls, greeting students by name, where members of the staff may be fluent in more than one language, and where the office staff is warm, and where students, in general, are mannerly. It is a school where students feel they have a part in running its day-to-day operation. It is a school that encourages discussion, cooperation, and teamwork. It is a school where people ask questions first and make decisions later. Perhaps it is a school where students run their morning television production in Spanish and Farsi, as well as English.

It is not a school community without conflict. Sometimes, it takes longer to get to a resolution on a thorny issue, because discussion and negotiation often take longer than edict. Sometimes—especially in the beginning—a few parents decide to move their children elsewhere. It is a school whose challenges include an ever-growing need for resources, a continuing struggle with adult ignorance and fear, and an ongoing battle to meet the academic standards of the majority community. But, almost always, it is a school that begins to hear the words "engaged," "vital," "interesting," "full of energy," and "successful" attached to its name.

The population of the United States has passed the 3 billion mark. Much of this growth is happening, not because people in our old communities are having more babies, but because of the growing numbers of newcomers who seek to build a life here. Public schools must educate the children. The choice is not whether, but how. We can be relevant, or not.

• • •

The diversity of the student body can add to the richness of the education of everyone in the school. But successfully leading such a community demands new skills, new sensitivity, and a new vocabulary. These can be developed through communication practices that address these common truths:

- The community, the school, and the home must be drawn together to support the child.

- School culture must remove, not build, barriers to community and parent involvement.
- Symbolism is important. Displaying flags representative of the home countries of student body is not only strikingly beautiful, but it sends a message about what you value.
- Information is power. Parents need easy access to facts. The community needs a vision.
- All parents have hopes and dreams for their children.

For reflection

1. Describe your role in promoting practices to address cultural differences.
2. What are some issues that contribute to your school's cultural competence?
3. Describe the symbols in your school environment that cue either cultural acceptance or serve as barriers to cultural coherence.

13

FACE THOSE ANGRY PARENTS

Turning a Complaint into a Gift

All substances are poison; there is none which is not a poison. The right dose differentiates a poison and a remedy.

—Paracelsus

"Oh, dear, here she comes again!"

"I am so tired of meeting with that group of parents. They never listen!"

"All the Smiths do is complain! Nothing is ever right! What jerks!"

Sound familiar? We suspect there are few offices in any school or school system that don't have a list of *least* favorite clients. Our tendency when we see them coming is to shut down, turn off, and look away. We avoid the unpleasant encounter whenever we can, but the hard truth is that, in doing so, we sometimes lose valuable opportunities to become a better organization and to create new advocates. We should rethink our strategy.

DISCLAIMER: SOME FOLKS ARE SIMPLY INTRACTABLE

It is important to say at the start that there are some people who simply refuse to engage. They are generally people whose objective is to create discord. They have no desire to reach peace. There is little or nothing that any of us can do to bring them on board. Trying becomes wasted effort on our part.

Our experience, however, is that there are very few of these people in our world. Most parents or neighbors or staff members who come to us with complaints are looking for something more—something better—and, if we are clever, we can enlist their help in creating that better thing. Those are the people we want to talk most about in this chapter.

MANAGING YOUR STAKEHOLDERS' EXPECTATIONS AND MAKING COMPLAINTS DISAPPEAR

We often forget to tell our stakeholders things that they should know. We forget to be clear about what our mission is, about what the limit of our skills is, and, equally important, about constraints on our resources. We just assume they understand. But they don't. If we haven't told them, they don't have access to important information. Without that information, stakeholders set expectations we simply can't meet.

Schools make rules ("Kindergarten parents are not allowed to walk their children to class after the first week of school," for instance). Often there are good reasons for these rules, but we forget to explain to parents what those reasons are. Inevitably, parents complain.

Employees see benefit changes on their pay stub and are angry because they don't understand. The superintendent assumed they were all listening to the discussion when the school board voted on the changes. (Doesn't everyone stay up late on Thursday evenings to watch school board meetings?) The superintendent didn't clearly explain the ramifications in his employee communications. The employees were left bewildered.

A principal takes heat for "insufficient" after-school staffing, because parents don't know that she has traded that budgeted staff time to gain an extra reading teacher. She didn't tell them.

Being abundantly clear about how the business of school is conducted, and why, makes stakeholders feel more secure—even if they don't agree with every decision. Their expectations become more realistic. Comfortable stakeholders complain less.

SAYING THANK YOU

For the sake of argument, let us assume that you do run a pretty open shop and you do take time to explain what is going on. Even so, Mrs. Campbell has called to make an appointment with you to share her complaint.

"When customers feel dissatisfied with products and services, they have two options: they can say something or they can walk away," say Janelle Barlow and Claus Moeller, authors and business consultants.

"If they walk away, they give organizations virtually no opportunity to fix their dissatisfaction." Complaining customers, on the other hand, "are still talking with us, giving us an opportunity to return them to a state of satisfaction. . . . So as much as we might not like to receive negative feedback, *customers who complain are giving us a gift*" (Barlow and Moeller, 1996, p. 8, italics added).

Further, they add, "listening to complaints is the equivalent of Native Americans who used to place their ears to the ground to hear distant hoof beats" (p. 4). If a few parents are upset, could there not be more who simply won't voice their feelings openly? Maybe you should be concerned about what is troubling them. The conflict may be larger than you thought. Listening might lead to new and creative solutions.

Your first statement, then, to Mrs. Campbell when she comes to your office should be "Thank you for bringing your concern to my attention." She has given you the opportunity, at the very least, to make your relationship with her better. She may have tipped you off to a bigger problem.

UNDERSTANDING THE ANGER

No one likes to listen to complaints. It is difficult to sit still while someone dumps a load of rage on your desk. It helps to understand why people get angry. Understanding may also help to shape the solution. According to those who study human behavior, there are some fundamental reasons why we get angry:

- *We get angry because we have been hurt, or because our children have been hurt.* This hurt can be physical or emotional. Your son gets decked in a playground fight, or your daughter is the subject of continuing ridicule by a teacher or another student. Your inquiries, as a parent, have been repeatedly ignored by your child's teacher. Those situations make us angry.

- *We get angry when we are afraid we WILL be hurt in the future.* Ever get up on the morning you have a dentist appointment and yell at your kids? You aren't angry at them, but your anxiety over the pain your dentist *might* inflict spills over. Parents get angry about their child's kindergarten teacher selection if they are already afraid their child might not get into Harvard.
- *We get angry when our fundamental values or beliefs are threatened.* In every school it's likely that someone's values and beliefs are threatened every day. As our communities grow more and more diverse, we must become more and more sensitive to cultures and religious practices that are different from our own, to other peoples' sense of personal space, and to our own use of language. We have no idea how often we offend without meaning too.
- *We get angry when we believe that we have been ignored or lied to or treated unfairly.* The people who can attest to this most vividly are the administrative assistants who answer the phones in our organization. The higher you go in the organization, the more layers there are to the stories they hear. By the time a complainant reaches the superintendent's or a school board member's office, not only is the parent or citizen complaining about the original insult, but also about the multiple attempts to discuss the problem that were met with silence, or worse, down the line. With time and repeated rebuffs, the "Johnny did not get into the gifted program" becomes "this whole school system is a disaster."

Parents' complaints can be a gift, and their persistence can sometimes expose a fundamental flaw in the organization's management (Suskind and Field, 1996).

IDENTIFYING STAKEHOLDERS' NEEDS

The needs of our stakeholders—parents, colleagues, community members—can be filed in one of three buckets. In our interactions with each other, we all need:

- *Security.* In any relationship, parents want to feel secure, and they want to be sure that their children are secure. We don't expect to be physically assaulted inside a school, and we also don't want to be verbally or emotionally assaulted in our dealings with school personnel.
- *Esteem.* Beyond feeling secure, our parents and our colleagues also want to be respected. Parents feel intimidated by the "professional" (arrogant?) attitude that educators sometimes adopt. Parents want to feel that their opinion is given weight in the process of building solutions. Colleagues too are put off when someone from another department or building knows it all!
- *Justice.* Finally, our stakeholders are looking for justice. Usually, we can accept a solution we don't like if it applies equally to everyone. When other people or children seem to be getting special treatment, temperatures rise and tempers flare. "That's just not fair," we say.

These three buckets match up pretty well with the things that make us angry. They give us clues to building constructive conversations with angry parents. Write those three words—security, esteem, justice—on a piece of paper and tape it to your phone. When you are listening to a complaining parent or employee, focus on which one best describes the complaint you are hearing. When it is your turn to talk, don't start addressing the problem, start with an acknowledgment of your understanding of the parent/employee need:

- "It sounds to me, Mrs. Quinn, as if you don't feel Suzanne is *safe*." Or
- "What you are telling me is that you believe that the principal is *not listening* to what you have to say." Or
- "Mr. Andretti, you seem to feel that your son is not being treated *fairly* by the coach."

Almost without fail, you will find that those simple sentences take much of the heat out of the conversation and give you and the complainant some breathing room in which to find a solution.

DELIVERING SERVICES SEAMLESSLY

Major companies across the country have spent considerable amounts of time, energy, and money devising and implementing good customer service models that include effective ways of receiving and responding to customer complaints. Ritz-Carlton Hotels is a leader in the field. The Ritz-Carlton says customers want a "seamless delivery of services." Parents don't care *how* the mistake (or perceived mistake) was made or *who* mishandled the request or *why* a promised deadline is missed. They want to be heard.

What Customers *Don't* Want

- Excuses
- Silence (no response at all)
- A denial of responsibility ("That's not in my job description.")
- Rude treatment ("Are you kidding?")
- Rejection ("We've never done that before!")
- Promises, not delivered ("We'll get right on it, trust me.")
- Being passed on ("Well, why don't you try the transportation department.")

The first things parents most want are pretty straightforward:

- A quick response. This is not necessarily a resolution, but it is the returned phone call and the acknowledgment that the issue exists and that it will be heard.
- An apology. This doesn't have to be an acknowledgment of wrongdoing. Perhaps there wasn't any. But it can be, "I can see that this has upset you and your family a great deal. I'm very sorry."
- Good information. After being a good listener, the next most important step to a satisfactory resolution is providing clear, pertinent information. Often people get angry when they feel helpless because they are unable to find the right information. Knowing the facts can sometimes change a response from negative to positive. Facts can reset expectations.

Your job when you hear the complaint is, first, to keep your own blood pressure down and then to listen carefully to the story you are hearing. Ask clarifying questions. Don't assume you know the answers. Listen for hidden clues and messages. (Is this family in the middle of a divorce? Is this child having a similar problem at Sunday School or at scout meetings? Are there veiled accusations of ethnic, religious, or racial prejudice in the conversation?) The presenting problem may not be the only issue.

As an active listener in the conversation, you have the opportunity to help clarify and define the problem. You certainly have the chance to defuse the anger and get closer to the real issues.

Why Customers Leave

- 1 percent die
- 3 percent move away
- 5 percent develop other relationships
- 9 percent leave for competitive reasons
- 14 percent are dissatisfied with produce
- 68 percent leave because of the poor way they were treated by employees

—Kirk Kazanjian

MOVING TOWARD A SOLUTION

What if you can't "fix" the situation? What if there is no real solution that will satisfy the parent? What you do depends on where you sit in the organization. If you are at or near the bottom, and you do not have the authority to change what the parent is asking to change, then helping that parent get to the person who does have authority is the customer friendly thing to do. (It's not "Why don't you call," but rather "Let me have my supervisor call you.") This, of course, assumes that you have a good working relationship with your supervisor!

If you are up the ladder, then it is your job to make the customer feel understood and to help him or her grasp what responses are possible. You and the customer work together to find the best option. It is a combination of education and diplomacy. If there simply is no satisfactory answer, or a decision is not going the customer's way, be sure that you call or meet personally to deliver the bad news. The only thing people hate worse than bad news is to be ignored.

Remember that these conversations do not take place in a vacuum. If a parent or employee or neighbor brings a complaint in a situation where the organization is already perceived as closed, negative, or hostile, then that person arrives already carrying a large chip. He or she is not expecting solutions, only rejection. If, however, your office is known as one that is open, reasonable, and collegial, the conversation begins with a decided bias toward shared resolution. How you have set the stage, day in and day out, in your dealings with all your stakeholders will influence the conclusion.

NO SURPRISES

Key to successful negotiation in difficult situations is having the best information possible. A father, full of frustration and indignation, told us his story:

> My little boy came home crying two days before Halloween and said that his teacher said that they couldn't wear their costumes to school on October 31 and there would be no party. He was heart-broken. There has ALWAYS been a party on Halloween at that school.
>
> I was outraged. I called the principal, and she said there was nothing she could do about it. Then I called the superintendent's office and got an answering machine. I left a really stinging message. How dare they! But no one ever called me back!

A colleague who overheard the story asked us later, "What could the superintendent, or anyone, have done?" Well, plenty.

- The first mistake someone made (we never heard the other side of the story) was to announce at the last moment a decision with that much emotional content without including parents in the process or at least being sure that all parents knew well ahead of the date that the rules were changing. (No surprises.)

- Parents should have been told why the decision was made, so that they understood and so that they could help their children understand. (No surprises.)
- If the decision was made at the school level, the principal should have anticipated that someone might still take their complaint forward, and the principal should have alerted the superintendent's office to the change. (No surprises.)
- The superintendent or an aide—armed with the right information—should have returned the call immediately. (Common courtesy.)

Suppose the principal had decided not to celebrate the event in school because the students need more class time. Suppose she had elicited parent support, had sent the decision to parents out in plenty of time, and had discussed the matter with the superintendent. Suppose the dad had missed or ignored her notification. How then might the phone call between the superintendent and the parent have gone?

The superintendent could have begun with a recognition of the student's real disappointment and the parent's subsequent disappointment. The superintendent could have reviewed how and why the decision was made. She could have said, "I understand that you may disagree with our choices, but we felt strongly that these children will have ample time and opportunity to celebrate Halloween with their friends and family after school, and that we needed to use this time for instruction."

It wasn't the answer the parent wanted, but perhaps it was one he could understand.

Everyone at all levels in the organization needs to be constantly on the alert for issues that might explode. And everyone needs to keep the leadership informed and ready. Having the information at hand—and not being surprised—means dealing from strength. No surprises.

RECOVERING SUCCESSFULLY

A complaining customer gives you a second chance. Industry research documents that if you succeed the *second* time with a customer—if you make good on your error or perceived error—you actually create a more memorable impression on the customer than if everything had gone smoothly the first time. Remember the Tylenol scare? It wasn't even a manufacturer error, but the company responded immediately by pulling the product off the shelves and won huge public support.

Often the most effective recovery takes place in the very first interaction between your angry parent and a staff member. Don't underestimate the importance of that encounter. "The content or form of the employee's response is what causes the customer to remember the event either favorably or unfavorably" (Suskind and Field, 1996, p. 109). It is important not only that you develop these skills, but that you help everyone down the line develop them too. Training for your administrative assistants may be one of the best steps that you can take.

HANDLING THE TOUGH COOKIES SKILLFULLY

Let's return now to those intractable folks we left at the beginning of this chapter, the ones we would *really* like never to meet again. What do we do when we see them coming?

First, protect your employees. We have already discussed how incivility in the workplace (employee to employee as well as customer to employee) has a huge negative effect in productivity and employee turnover (Pearson and Porath, 2005).

It is important for your staff members to understand that while being polite to customers and colleagues is the standard, it does not mean that they must suffer abuse from a parent or another employee. It is important for employees to know that they have support and backup in really difficult situations. Have a plan to handle these situations and be sure that all your staff members understand how to execute it.

MEDIATING FOR YOURSELF

Once tempers have cooled a bit, you may find yourself sitting down across the table from this parent or group of parents. The problems still need to be addressed. This is when you turn to real mediation tactics. If a situation has festered a long time, or the stakes are too high for a local solution, you may need to call in a mediation team. Perhaps there are counselors or psychologists in your organization, trained in mediation skills, on whom you can call.

But perhaps this is an issue that you can handle yourself with some careful planning. Coleman McCarthy, a former writer for the *Washington Post*, is the founder of the Center for Teaching Peace. He now spends much of his professional life teaching mediation and conflict resolution to young people. Here is some of his advice:

- "Listen. This is one of the hardest things to do. Let people finish their sentences. Listening is showing respect.
- "Deal with facts, not opinions. Don't ask, 'What happened?' That question elicits only *opinion*. Ask instead, 'What did you do?' That will get you *facts*.
- "It's never *you* against *me*. It's always you *and* me against the issue. Frame the questions so that everyone is on the same side. That starts you off closer to the solution.
- "Line up all the things you and they have in common against the *one* thing on which you don't agree.
- "Always hold your peace talks away from the scene of the battle. (The treaty with the British that ended the American Revolution was signed in Paris.) People are calmer when they are not looking at the blood on the floor." (McCarthy, n.d.)

WALKING AWAY WITH A NEW PARTNER

Don't write off the jerks in your school system. Decide instead to build new relationships and come away from each conflict with some new friends. Vow to create solutions together, no matter how long it takes.

While you are dealing with those complainants whose gifts are hard to discern, look again at the systems you have in place that encourage regular, honest feedback from your employees and your stakeholders. Is your ear continually to the ground? Or does it take an earthquake to get your attention? The more you listen, the easier listening will be.

• • •

Angry parents—and staff members, for that matter—can become valuable members of your team. By coming to you, they offer you the chance to rebuild a damaged relationship, and they may be an early warning of a larger problem of which you were not aware. Learn to address these folks in a respectful and productive way. You may just turn them into staunch allies.

For reflection

1. How can you work with staff to improve your response to complaining customers?
2. What complaints have you heard in the last month that might lead you to better service?
3. Do you anticipate the issues and decisions that will raise issues for your customers? Have you managed your customers' expectations as well as possible?

(14)

DAZZLE THE 80 PERCENT

Reaching Out to the Larger Community

If you really want to help this world, what you have to teach is how to live in it.

—Joseph Campbell

Remember our discussion about the majority of people in communities who pay taxes but do not have school-aged children? Too many school districts ignore these folks most of the time and appeal to them only when it is time to pass a school levy or a bond referendum. Historically, schools have kept their perimeters pretty tight—sort of a "green zone" in the middle of town—arguing that it is "too much trouble" to mess with community affairs, and what's going on in schools "is really none of their business anyway."

Schools cite the stress of having political candidates wanting to use their classrooms as backdrops for ads or campaigning at back-to-school night. Teachers dislike having community classes or night school in their classrooms because "equipment gets broken" or "materials disappear." Varsity coaches are reluctant to share playing fields with the local recreation department because the grass gets torn up or the gates are not properly locked after the game.

We do not underestimate these difficulties. We too have faced down candidates and elected officials who have tried to bully their way into classrooms during school hours. We have watched a community where schools and local government officials negotiated for over a year to arrive at an equitable facilities-use agreement.

What we would argue, however, is that school leaders need to take a larger view of their relationship with the communities of which they are a part. Our lives as schools and school districts are intricately intertwined with the fabric of our communities. Rather than turn our backs, we must capitalize on these connections.

LOCAL CONCERNS PERMEATE SCHOOL AIR

We have already talked about the impact that community issues can have on schools. Despite all their efforts to stay apart, schools do not exist in isolation. If parents in the community struggle over what freedoms to allow their children, schools may see heated debates on family life education or suffer challenges to the books sitting on library shelves. If there are race and class concerns in the community, schools may experience pressure to increase the numbers of honors and gifted and talented classes. If the community is torn by hostility over issues of illegal immigration or the presence of gangs, the schools are sure to be drawn in. There is no way to keep schools out of the discussion.

TURNING THE EQUATION ON ITS HEAD

Given that schools are inevitably linked to their community, we suggest that school leaders use these issues and interruptions to instruction as opportunities to broaden their school's or school system's influence and gain new friends and supporters. (We know there is precious little time. But a whole school board meeting given to the discussion of book challenges takes precious time too.)

When school leaders do not engage in community issues that impinge upon students, or—in the absence of any major issue—when they simply ignore the larger community, a black cloud of questions and doubt gathers overhead. "What are those schools up to?" taxpayers ask. Leaders, on the other hand, who meet community challenges head-on with a cooperative and open spirit gain the trust of those external stakeholders—the 80 percent.

More than one elementary principal has spent a whole year at neighborhood morning coffees with preschool moms, to stem the flight to private schools. More than one superintendent has created advisory panels of Latino or African American parents to train effective advocates for students often underrepresented—and in doing so, turned agitators into advocates. After 9/11, more than one superintendent in northern Virginia, and elsewhere, created an advisory committee composed of Muslim clerics and prominent citizens of Middle Eastern heritage to work toward better cultural understanding among students and adults in schools.

Whether you are trying to breach cultural or racial differences or build support for a comprehensive, on-site, after-school program, you, as school leader, are once again trying to shift the paradigm. You are once again leading change, and, to be successful, you will have to change opinions both inside and outside school walls. In fact, you must reposition the school in its relationship to the community—not isolated at the top of the hill, but right down in the heart of town.

Often, when we want to change things—because we are educators and live much of the time in our heads—we expend a good deal of effort providing research and critical information to our stakeholders so that they can understand the issue. We make a convincing argument with facts and figures. We figure if people have the information, they will make the right decision.

In truth, to lead this kind of community-connected change, you need to do much more. You must

- *Meet your stakeholders where they are.* Take your message to the streets. (Remember Ned Lamont?) For too long, school leaders have expected citizens to come to them and ask for information. Making the argument at a single evening meeting at the high school will not turn the tide.
- *Reframe the situation into a win-win.* This is about getting to yes. Schools can no longer say, "The city budget is all about *us*." The police and firemen will make the same argument. So will the senior citizens. It's really about the whole community. We need to make the case that helping schools will help the whole community.

- *Find the emotional hook and articulate the urgency that will move people to action.* "People change when they are emotionally engaged and committed" says scholar and author Daniel Goleman. What makes leadership effective "is finding passion for the work, for the strategy, and for the vision—and engaging hearts and minds." He concludes, "When leaders engage only on an intellectual level, it's virtually impossible to maintain energy and commitment" (Goleman, 2002, p. 239). Our work *is* about the children and there *is* an urgency to this matter. Use it.

- *Offer members of the community a new experience of the schools.* Most citizens have not been in a school in many years—not since they graduated or since their last-born graduated. Their notions of what we do are often antiquated. Schools have changed. We need to *demonstrate* that change. Show, not tell. (If you can't travel to the Arctic, pictures and artifacts can help you understand what it *feels* like to be there.)

Compromises are often born out of collisions.

—Brian Williams, NBC *Nightly News*

One community was facing a massive redistricting involving six high schools. Building renovations could not keep pace with the population shifts from one end of the county to the other, and, as a result, some schools had become severely overcrowded, while others had seats to spare. The empty seats were located mainly in older neighborhoods that had become far more culturally and economically diverse than the newer developments. All the schools sent graduates on to the best universities, but the community battle over the proposed boundary lines was in danger of becoming class warfare.

Students at one of the high schools with empty seats decided to step out and make their case. They formed teams and launched a marketing campaign, targeting parents whose children might be placed in their school under the new plan. These students wanted to persuade the skeptics by countering, with their presence, the rumors on the streets about their student body and their academic standing. They spoke at a series of PTA meetings and invited the parents for the neighboring communities to come and visit the school. According to the *Washington Post* coverage (November 18, 2007) of their initiative, the students were somewhat disappointed by the reception they received. But if their campaign was not wildly successful, it was not because they did the wrong thing. We can learn from their marketing savvy.

MAKING CHOICES

Building relationships with community stakeholders, like building all other kinds of relationships, is an ongoing business. It's a process, not an endpoint. And like other processes, you have to start by making choices. In any given year, in any given school district, you can't take care of all your relationships equally. You have to be a good steward of your person power and your resources.

The needs of your community may dictate where you start. The leadership of Hamilton High School, in Sussex, Wisconsin, decided they wanted to strengthen their connections with older citizens in their community. They looked at the school's resources and the senior community's needs and found a match. The seniors wanted an indoor facility for walking exercise during the winter months. (Remember, this is Wisconsin!) Three times around the halls of the main floor at Hamilton High equals one mile.

The school launched a program to win the hearts and minds of their neighbors. They sent a letter to senior walkers in the community inviting them to walk on four evenings a week or during three ninety-minute blocks of time during the day when students were in class. They included a floor plan showing the route, the distance, and a school calendar marked with the dates when the school would be closed for holidays. They also attached a brochure for their *Seniors & Students Program*, which recruits and trains senior volunteers as tutors and aides in the high school. The brochure quoted Erma Bombeck, a familiar voice to that generation: "Volunteers are the only human beings on the face of this earth who reflect this nation's compassion, unselfish caring, patience, and just plain loving one another."

In one stroke the school reached out to a key stakeholder group, paid them a huge compliment, offered a service, and asked for their support (actually, another compliment). A win-win-win.

"Our walkers plan their day [around the times] that they can walk," reports Denise Lindberg, the public information and volunteer coordinator for the district. She recounts how, when one senior was no longer able to walk, his wife regularly pushed him through the halls in his wheelchair so that they could continue to greet the students.

"Several of our senior walkers have grandchildren who attend the high school, and they like the opportunity to have a chance encounter with one of them," Lindberg continued. One walker made friends with the school social worker and learned about the difficulties that some of the students faced at home. That walker, also a quilter, decided that she could help by making quilts for these kids in trauma. It was her way of "giving each of the children a hug at a time when they needed it most."

AUDIENCE OR ISSUE?

You could just as easily decide to work with neighborhood associations, your business community, preschool families, or the health care workers. Where is there friction with your school or district? Where is there misinformation? Whose support do the schools need? In communication lingo, this is called "segmenting your audience." It is a recognition, not only of the limits of your resources, but also of the fact that not everyone in the community wants or needs the same attention. Your neighbors may be worried only about the impact of the new school construction. Citizens on fixed incomes may only want to know that the tax increases they are being asked to bear are not being squandered.

If you don't start with a particular audience, you can start with an issue. Did gang tags show up on school buildings recently? Is there general unhappiness in the community with how the schools call snow days? Is there a community buzz about the gap in test scores between the minority and majority student populations? Any of these topics can give you a launching pad—as can happy news, like the naming of a Blue Ribbon School.

In northern Virginia, where the housing market usually remains relatively hot (we turn people out with every national election cycle!), the attitudes of realtors can have a huge effect on schools in all the jurisdictions. We did some investigating and discovered that there was no consistent flow of accurate school information to our local real estate companies. We found that some agents used school websites, but many relied on rumor and old statistics to make recommendations to their clients. (Technically, agents are not supposed to make any school recommendations, only supply data; but there was too much anecdotal evidence to the contrary for us to feel confident they were following regulations. Even the incoming superintendent, who did not disclose his identity, was steered by an agent away from neighborhoods whose schools she considered "bad.")

So, we met with a small group of realtors and asked what information was helpful for them to have for their clients. We beefed up our district website so that they could find that information easily, and we created rack cards, directing folks to the website—cards that were simple and inexpensive to print in large quantities.

The Northern Virginia Association of Realtors has a major showcase and association luncheon once a year. Vendors from many allied industries—roofers, mortgage brokers, moving companies—exhibit. As a result of our discussions with the realtors, the association offered us a booth at the expo. We hung posters with great pictures of winsome kids and set up laptops to demo our district website. We had general print information about the system and pencils to hand out. We staffed the booth, not only with members of the communications department, but also with a rotation of senior-level district administrators. The agents got to meet the real people who run the schools. Hundreds of realtors stopped by the booth, and many thanked us for helping them understand how to find current information. The association was as happy as we were with the results, and we returned the next year and the next.

We met the industry on its own turf. We gave them information they needed to get their job done. Instead of bashing them for their school bashing, we reframed the topic to a win-win (they got what they needed, and, armed with new tools, ceased to perpetuate old rumors). They met school people whom they found they liked (the emotional component). And they saw the schools reaching out—a new experience for many of them.

> If I marketed my business the way you [market your schools], I'd have no business. Quit talking about your deficiencies and start talking about what you are doing right.
>
> —Businessman, Witchita, KS (Bagin, 2007c, p. 15)

REACHING THE HARD TO REACH

Whether you begin by issue or by stakeholder group, the sad truth is that most of the people in the community will fall through the cracks in your plan. Probably 80 percent of the 80 percent are hard to find by the kinds of targeted marketing we have just described. So, if you are to spread your influence even further, you may have to work even harder—or smarter.

The old way to reach the whole community was to do a mass mailing to every home. Very time intensive—and, these days, very expensive. But school systems are full of clever folks inventing clever solutions. Some of the methods we have seen them use to reach a broad audience include:

- Web. The school, or school system, website is a key place for getting messages out to the school community. Linking the school website to other sites (like the government or neighborhood sites) can be useful in reaching nonschool families.
- Television. School systems that have their own cable channels produce public-information programming and even PSA messages that appear on other cable channels. Schools without their own channel use the community cable channel bulletin board to announce upcoming events of interest to citizens.
- Newspapers. Some school systems buy ads or negotiate pro bono ads in local papers—particularly in the annual "education edition." Letters to the editor from key community leaders who are school supporters can help clarify difficult issues. Buying an insert in the regular edition can be a relatively inexpensive print solution that will reach many nonschool homes.
- Joint programs. A growing number of school systems have created school-community scholarship foundations to raise money to support deserving local graduates on their way to postsecondary education. These programs not only provide needed financial help for the students, but also are a great way for the community to learn about, and invest in, the academic success of the school system.
- Citizen groups. Neighborhood associations are active in many communities and are full of people concerned about what is going on locally. The care and feeding of neighborhood associations and

other like groups is a great way to keep connected. Principals and superintendents who sit on these boards and make regular presentations have a strong presence in the community.

- Neighborhood blogs. We have mentioned these new-tech creatures before. More and more blogs are carrying the local news. Perhaps your school(s) should be part of the conversation.
- Bus posters. School systems have negotiated with local bus companies for donated space for school ads—both inside the bus and on the sides and back.
- Radio. Here is another outlet for PSA announcements and/or programming. This medium is particularly effective at targeting individual segments of a community.
- Principals' or superintendents' advisory councils. These groups can include representatives from local civic groups who can be key communicators back to their own flocks. These folks can also provide the superintendent with good counsel on current community school gossip. We know a principal who established *two* parent advisory committees—one that meets in the morning and one that meets in the evening after work to accommodate citizens' schedules.

Each of these tactics works better with some messages than with others, and better in some communities than in others. Your job as leader—with your team—is to sort through all the available options and decide which will get *your* message out to the people you want to reach in the easiest way possible. Whatever means you choose, however, be sure that you are timely. *Nothing* infuriates citizens—or parents and employees, for that matter—more than receiving notice too late to respond. An e-mail invitation or a news release that arrives the same day as the event is *not acceptable*.

"Have a little respect!" one irate father exclaimed! "I'll do my best to be there—but I need a little time to plan!" He's absolutely right.

KEEPING IT SIMPLE

Not every outreach initiative must be elaborate. Perhaps the children of one elementary school make holiday greeting cards for residents of the retirement home next door. Perhaps the high school art department arranges a show at the local art league or the drama department provides tickets to their spring play through the recreation department. Perhaps with city and school staff members together arrange a series of informational meetings on community issues that affect children, such as obesity, drugs, or violence. The effect of such small steps is cumulative and profound.

As important as the information and the messages that you convey by all this work is, what really matters is that citizens in the community meet schools and school students and employees in new and up-close ways. What matters is that citizens see schools as inquisitive, open, welcoming institutions that are a working part of the community. Then, when budget time comes, the neighbors will not clamor for the school funding to be cut, but will see the schools' contribution as adding value to the whole town.

Effective leaders, says Daniel Goleman, "have genuine passion for their mission and that passion is contagious. Their enthusiasm and excitement spread spontaneously, invigorating those they lead" (Goleman, Boyatzis, and McKee, 2002, p. 248). We show our enthusiasm to our employees. We show it to our parents. We must also show it to the community. Sharing that passion with the 80 percent is a vital part of our mission.

• • •

In many of our communities, 80 percent of the citizens do not have children in the public schools. In order to maintain the support of the community, we must be sure that that these citizens have accurate information about the schools and feel a connection to the schools and their success. School leaders must be creative in finding ways to cultivate those connections, using any means available—including personal contact, facility use, and volunteer programs. It's a matter of finding ways to share the passion!

For reflection

1. What school-community connections are already working in your neighborhood? How can you capitalize on their strengths?

2. What can you learn from school-community programs that have crashed and burned?
3. What are the top three school issues simmering in your community?
4. Who might you bring together to help you focus on an issue and design a response initiative?

IV

THE CRISIS

15

THINK SMART UNDER FIRE

Mastering Basic Crisis Communications

Everybody has a strategy until they get hit in the mouth.

—Mike Tyson

Nowhere will you see the payoff for your hard work building relationships and establishing connections more clearly than on the day that you are faced with a critical incident in your school or school system—a fire, a death, a tornado, or an employee conviction for sexual abuse. When the going gets tough, it is the relationships that you have built over time—with your staff members, parents, neighbors, business partners, and your community—that become the currency on which you draw.

Street wisdom says there are two kinds of school leaders in this world: those who have faced a crisis and those who are about to. Those of you who have had the parking lot filled with television trucks with their telescoping satellite dishes understand how critical the support of your employees and your community is in those moments. The rest of you read on, as an act of faith.

Planning and practice are crucial for effective crisis management, but every critical incident that you will face will be different. Among the most important leadership qualities that you bring to each situation are *flexibility* and *creativity*. You must be prepared, and you must also be ready to improvise. Crisis management is the practice of common sense at the speed of light, but you cannot assume that the people with whom you work will always exhibit common sense in times of stress. That part is your task as a leader.

Effective leadership in critical incidents can be roughly divided into three parts:

- Crisis preparation and management—what you do to protect the safety of your staff and students
- Crisis communication—how you tell your stakeholders what's happening and what the school and school district are doing to respond
- Crisis intervention and support—how, during the crisis and afterward, you help everyone involved make sense of what has happened and regain a sense of normalcy

These three disciplines go hand in hand. How you communicate during a crisis can shape the events and the outcome of the crisis. But communication alone will not be enough to solve the issue. So, before we talk about communications, a brief look at crisis management and support.

CRISIS MANAGEMENT

Most school systems have a number of resources upon which school leaders can draw to help them deal with a critical incident. Among them are

- Regulations that delineate internal chain of command and duties in a crisis
- Protocols for school evacuation, lockdown, shelter-in-place, and student-parent reunification
- An internal school security team
- A district community-relations officer or communications team
- School resource officers from the local police department
- A good working relationship with local public safety officials

Leading a crisis management team means that the safety and well-being of students and employees is your first responsibility. Whatever it takes. You need to know who is empowered to make a decision to evacuate or lock down and have careful plans for communicating that decision to the school or entire school division. In a real emergency, you may have less than a minute to move forward. Even though public safety support may arrive quickly, you may not be able to wait. When an incident happens, there is no time to go to the shelf and read the regulations or look up key phone numbers. Those things need to be in your head.

Be Prepared
Here's how your competence will be judged after the crisis passes:

- Were you able to assess the situation accurately?
- Did you respond quickly?
- Did you have the required background knowledge at your fingertips?
- Did stakeholders feel informed and confident in your work?

It is in the first minutes that you may be the only one calling the shots. Once the police, fire, or hazmat team is on-site, pubic safety officials will be in charge of the site and will begin to make decisions about the management of the incident. Your role then changes to one of support.

It is for those few minutes that you prepare. The first assessment of danger and the immediate call to lock down or evacuate is yours. It is important to create crisis response teams in schools, in departments, and at the district level to support you. Teams at every level need to plan and practice a series of crisis responses—to a gas leak, a hurricane, an intruder, a roof collapse, a suicide. There are a growing number of crisis response resources available to schools and districts, many of them online. The U.S. Department of Education's disaster preparedness site is a good place to start. Check with your state department of education and your sister school divisions as well.

Ask your security department or your local police department to run tabletop training exercises for your staff. In these workshops you and your team are presented with a scenario and asked to walk through the steps you would take to respond. This is the kind of mental training that Olympic athletes use to prepare for competition. It is gold-medal preparation.

Once the school year gets under way, it is sometimes hard to carve out time to plan for situations that may seem remote, especially when instructional or operational decisions are pressing. "That will never happen here," we say. But it does. Find the time.

CRISIS SUPPORT

In the beginning moments of a critical incident, everyone runs on adrenaline. Nature gave us that fight or flight response for a reason, to get us through safely. But at some point you will begin to notice the signs of emotional bruising in yourself and in others—especially if the critical event and its resolution unfold over more than an hour or two. Students may become anxious or tearful. Adults may become forgetful or resentful, or simply don't show up to do jobs they have been assigned. The longer the crisis lasts, the deeper the wounds.

Ignore these signs of distress at your own peril. A former student was shot and killed on a high school parking lot as he tried to seek shelter inside the building. Several classes of students and their teachers witnessed the shooting from their classroom windows. The event happened in February. The next fall, the principal told us that the faculty and students had worked very hard to hold the school together through June. But over the next summer, the principal said, a record number of teachers resigned because of illness or requested transfer to other schools. "I underestimated the emotional damage," she said.

School leaders are very good at taking care of others, especially students. They often don't do so well at taking care of themselves. Build relief for yourself and your staff members into your emergency plans. That means knowing in detail who will take over key jobs when a staff member collapses or just needs a break.

Over the last ten years some key work has been done both inside and outside the educational community on posttraumatic stress and the components of effective crisis intervention. There are many simple things that can be done in a school community—short term and long term—that will help both students and adults deal with the aftereffects of trauma and build a new sense of normal. School counselors, psychologists, and social workers are the folks to lead this initiative. It is your job to empower them to do what they do best—get everyone back on their feet.

CRISIS COMMUNICATION

Once, long ago, we had an opportunity to plan and execute a crisis communication plan without a single interruption. Early one morning, we got a call from an elementary principal who had just received word from the local health department that one of her kindergarten students had been diagnosed with bacterial meningitis (that's the bad kind). The previous weekend a local high school student had been stricken and died within days. The newspapers had given the story a lot of ink. The community was on alert.

"Have the health department meet us at the school," we said, as we headed for the car. We sat down with the principal and the public health nurse in the school conference room at 8:45 a.m.

We knew that the morning kindergarten classes would be released at 11:00 a.m. We had two hours to work before the news would be on the street.

For the first hour, we made lists of what needed to be done to protect students and staff members who might have been exposed to the disease. We decided who needed to know what information and in what order they should be told. Parents of the children in the young girl's class had to be notified individually first. The faculty needed clear information. Then the PTA leadership needed to be alerted. All the parents in the school needed to hear from the school as quickly as possible. Beyond that, the division leadership and the school board needed to be briefed. But *we* wanted to be the one to tell the story to the press, so that it would be clear that the school was on top of the issue. No leaks. The timing was critical.

With an hour left before dismissal we drew up a timeline, gathered support troops, and began to write the communications: a letter to parents, a media release, talking points for the office staff to use as they responded to phone calls. Health department aides began calling the sixteen families who were most likely to be affected. A brief note was sent to all faculty just before the kindergarten dismissal outlining the situation and calling for a full faculty meeting with health department officials at the close of the school day. The principal briefed the superintendent, who then called school board members.

At 11:00, the kindergarten students filed to their buses with a carefully worded letter to parents in hand. At 11:10 a.m. a media release was faxed to the press. By 11:30 a.m., after the children had cleared the parking lot, we were on the sidewalk doing stand-ups with local television crews.

Calm and Available

That story broke just as we wanted it to. The newspapers and television reported:

- A case of meningitis has appeared.
- School and health department are working together.
- Parents and staff members have been informed.
- The community is calm.

That time, all the pieces were in place: a terrific principal, strong staff, a healthy relationship between the school and community, a good working relationship with the health department, a little time, and a lot of luck. (In the end, this child recovered, and there were no further cases in the town that year.)

You can't count on things happening that smoothly every time. Often there is an interruption, an early leak to the press—with students carrying cell phones these days, you are lucky if you have thirty minutes—or some other unexpected roadblock. Your success depends on your being flexible and being able to think on your feet.

It is hard to overestimate your role as leader during a critical incident. It is also hard to overestimate the importance of the way in which you communicate information about what's happening (to the best of your understanding) and how the school is responding. Think of the leaders that we have watched in crisis: Rudy Giuliani on-site on 9/11 became an instant symbol.

- They appear calm, clear, engaged thinkers.
- They are on the scene, assessing the situation, consoling the distraught, offering hope and solutions.
- They act quickly and decisively, but they rely heavily on the wisdom of the people around them. They work well with the public safety response team.
- They communicate, communicate, communicate. They meet with their stakeholders.

- They are accessible to the media. They keep public officials up to date.

Assuming your district has a communications team, you will be working closely together to craft your messages. There should be only one message and one messenger representing the school division. But even if the spokesman in front of the camera is not you, this is a moment when your staff members, your students, your parents, and the community beyond will be looking to you for strength. It is a moment for confidence and transparency. It is the moment to regularly and consistently put out the best information you have. Most of us, at one time or another, have worried whether or not we would have the "right stuff" under pressure. That kind of doubt, like stage fright, should fuel your preparations and make you better yet.

Grace under Pressure

Leaders must develop unique attributes to deal effectively with a crisis:

Steadiness. Rock-hard concentration is imperative.
Stamina. Crises can last for hours or days. Those involved must accommodate fatigue and retain their responsive edge.
Sensitivity. Understanding the people, politics, and problems involved is key. Each audience will have its own needs.

Clear and Steady

In October 2002, the Washington, D.C., metropolitan area was held hostage for three weeks by the shooting rampage of two men who were dubbed "the snipers." At the time, Fairfax County Public Schools (FCPS) was testing a fledgling push e-mail communication system called Keep-in-Touch. Anyone could register on the division's website to receive e-mail notices about a variety of issues—school lunches, school board meetings, special education, *and* emergencies.

During the harrowing weeks in which the snipers roamed and killed throughout the region, area school systems tried to keep a very low profile. We tried *not* to call attention to ourselves or our students. We tried *not* to be the subject of stories in the local papers, though all of the media wanted to cover how we were protecting the schools. At the same time, however, we needed desperately to stay connected with our parents who were understandably anxious. It was a difficult time in part because there was little that parents could *do* except read the paper, watch television news, and worry.

So the FCPS communications office devised a routine deliberately meant to be calming by its consistency. Using the division's website emergency page and the Keep-in-Touch e-mail notification—read mostly by parents—we put out regular updates on school actions at 10 a.m. and 4 p.m. each day. These updates included such things as the decision to bring all recess activities indoors, changes in the athletic schedules, and new procedures for dropping off and picking up students at the beginning and end of the day. A regularly updated "crawl" on the bottom of the division's public information cable station—which we determined might be more widely viewed—carried more general information.

By the end of the siege, our Keep-in-Touch subscriber base had quadrupled. More importantly, the superintendent heard over and over again from parents that receiving regular messages, even though there might not be much new information, had helped them feel confident in the school division's ability to take care of their children. Despite everyone's stress, relationships between school and home held.

The rapid advances in technology now make e-mail itself begin to look something like the Model T. During the shootings at Virginia Tech in 2007, it was to instant messaging that the students turned for information and direction. Tomorrow, another communication tool will most likely appear. This makes the school system's communication role difficult and expensive. But this readiness has become part of parent and community expectation.

Unintended Consequences

Three days into his new job, a high school principal guided his school through a suspected hazmat incident in a chemistry lab. Students were evacuated to the football stadium and eventually bussed home. Several students were sent to the hospital with possible complications of a suspected exposure. All day long, men in white space suits went in and out of the building. Police and firefighters held the perimeter, and members of the press roamed the grassy crescent in front of the main entrance, interviewing anyone they could. The principal was everywhere, talking to parents, consoling students, collaborating with public safety officials, giving interviews to reporters.

Many hours later, it was determined that no one had been exposed to any dangerous chemical. At the end of the day, the principal sat in his office, exhausted but clearly relieved that no one had been injured.

This principal had just succeeded a very popular principal who had had a long and successful run at the school. Now, after this chaos, he wondered if anyone would take him seriously.

"You don't understand, Henry," we told him, "today *established* you as the school's leader. You could have spent months trying to fill an old pair of boots, but after your work today, no one will ever question your right to sit in this office."

Henry did have a long and happy run as principal. (Remember, that Chinese character for *crisis* also means "opportunity.")

If you are lucky, you won't have to manage a crisis very often. If you do, at the end of the day, when everyone has finally left and you can at last draw a complete breath, you will probably *never* be able to look back and say, "Wow! We sure did that one right! Everything just fell into place." Critical incidents don't play like that. Stuff always happens that you are not planning on—like the network server goes down just when you need to send an urgent message to parents. What you want to be able to feel as you settle into your chair is that you and your staff did the best that you could, kept the children and the staff members as safe as possible, and didn't get in the way of good things happening tomorrow. That's enough.

• • •

In today's world no school or school system should be without a well-thought-out and well-practiced three-part crisis plan: including crisis preparation and management management, crisis communication, and crisis intervention. Clear and timely messages from the leader to all the affected stakeholders become more important than ever in a critical event.

For reflection

1. When was the last time you dusted off your crisis plan?
2. Does it need updating?

3. Do the newer members of your staff know the plan?
4. Have you included all the appropriate public safety and health officials in the plan? Do they have a copy?
5. How often do you practice?

A CASE STUDY IN CRISIS COMMUNICATIONS

Revisiting Our Assumptions

Critical incidents are those events in leaders' lives that offer the chance to improvise while still staying true to the script.

—James M. Kouzes and Barry Z. Posner

Little more than three months after the tragic deaths of thirty-three students and faculty members at Virginia Tech in April 2007,[1] sixty local reporters and editors gathered with spokespersons from the university, the student body, the state police force, and nearby school divisions. They met at the campus student center, only a block from where most of the shootings occurred, for a daylong conference assembled by the Associated Press of Virginia. The purpose of the seminar was to discover together what lessons could be learned from the communication and the reporting that occurred both during and after the event.

In welcoming the group, Mayor Ron Rordam of Blacksburg, where the university is located, spoke about how deeply the town had been touched by the incident.

"Even the city bus drivers kept working beyond their shifts that day to get everyone where they needed to be," he said. "The impact of this loss will be with us for years and years to come."

Talk at the meeting covered topics as broad as the spacious and well-groomed Tech campus: how the university officials managed the flow of information, how the editors had made their headline decisions, how everyone involved had dealt with their own emotions—or not—while working fifteen- to twenty-hour days. A Virginia Tech journalism professor and six of his students, who were together compiling a book about the event, spoke about their work (Lazenby, 2007).

More than half of the group had known someone who had died. A great undertow of sadness washed through the room. Everyone was trying to make sense of their collective experience.

By the end of the day, remarkable and instructive patterns emerged—some patterns that linked this tragedy to many of the other school tragedies we have witnessed and other patterns that set this event apart. In recent years, communities in this country and elsewhere have needed all too many after-action reviews such as this one—but these repeated looks give us new and important information about what to expect if we are ever to play a leadership role in a crisis.

THE MORE THINGS STAY THE SAME

Themes that seem to run through all stories of school tragedies emerged again in Blacksburg.

- *No one involved is ever the same again*. Everyone—no matter how stoic at the moment of impact—walks away changed. Everyone will grieve differently—some immediately, some not for months or years, some publicly, some only in their own soul. A bond will grow among "those who were there," and the rest of the world will always be outsiders.
- *There will be great anger*. Everyone will experience it in some way, at some time. The enormity, the unfairness, the unexpectedness, the injustice, the loss will overwhelm and turn itself into anger. The anger can be directed at many—and sometimes seemingly random—targets: the perpetrator (if there was one), God, the administration, the law enforcement community, the media. Anyone can feel the brunt.

- *There will be huge and honest differences of opinion about how to move forward.* At Virginia Tech, there were questions about whether or not the shooter (who was also a student and who took his own life) should be included in the prayers and memorials. The editors of the local papers disagreed about which pictures should appear on the front page and how large they should be. University and law enforcement officials struggled with how much information could be released to the public without jeopardizing the investigation. There were many opinions, coming from everywhere, about how best to honor the dead.
- *Time boundaries disappear.* When you are working in the middle of an event, you will put down the phone and look up at the clock to discover that five (or ten) hours have passed since your last touch with time. You have little thought about food or rest or your family or even a trip to the bathroom. This is important to remember because such behavior, over time, is not healthy for you or those working beside you. You are in this mess for the long haul. You need to monitor your personal resources, and that of your colleagues and staff, so that you minimize collapse. You will need reinforcements too.
- *The crisis plan that you worked so long and hard to create, and practice, will get scuttled.* Even the U.S. Army declares that "No plan survives initial contact with the enemy." Decisions will be made based on the situation as it develops. Flexibility and creativity will be essential leadership skills. (This does not mean that your planning work was in vain. You needed that preparation to teach your brain what to look for and to sharpen your decision-making skills. You needed the preparation to give you a framework within which to be flexible.)
- *There will be big, and sometimes ugly, surprises.* No matter how many contingencies you prepare for, there will be others. The cell phone service will crash. People will show up with political agendas. Virginia Tech spokesman, Larry Hincker, said that at first he felt overwhelmed by "the speed with which the information comes at you. It was like drinking from a fire hose." The video that the shooter sent to NBC in New York, and that the network subsequently aired, surprised and shocked everyone. "It had a devastating

effect on the morale of everyone on campus," commented a state official. No one saw that coming.

- *You will lose people in the aftermath*, sometimes just for an afternoon, sometimes for a long time. Some folks will be so distraught they simply won't show up for work. Some lose all sense of balance. Robert Bowman, managing editor of *Collegiate Times*, the Virginia Tech student newspaper, told of having to banish one young woman from the newsroom. She had lost friends in the incident and was trying to deal with her grief by working twenty-hour days. "We had to send her home," he said.

- *No matter how good your communication is, many hurtful and harmful rumors will crop up.* Some of them will travel quickly across the nation. You will not be able to squelch them all. Triage will be the skill needed to sort for the worst. "It was like playing Whack-A-Mole," recalled Corrine Geller, the Virginia State Police Public Relations Manager. "The minute you batted one rumor down, another popped up." At Tech these rumors ranged from initial reports that the shooter was a Chinese national who had just landed at LAX to claims that his family, living in Fairfax County, Virginia, had all committed suicide. Each rumor takes valuable time to trace down and refute.

- *Recovery—both for the organization and for the individual participants—is a balancing act.* From tragedy to tragedy, it seems that there are roles that must be filled for the event to play out. It is as if a basic script were handed out after each tragedy. All of the parts are important and need to be respected. Your job as the leader is to find ways to negotiate among these players and fit them all together into a workable unit. It is not an easy job. Every day the balance is likely to tip in a different direction. This is not necessarily a bad thing. You just need to pay attention.

  a. The lead investigators. These might be members of the local police, the state police, the FBI, the Federal Transportation Safety Board—depending on the particular event. It is their job to take charge of the scene and to find out what went wrong. Their chief line will be "We cannot release any information until we have all the facts. We will not speculate about what happened. We are not making any statement." Investigators cannot afford to make mistakes. They cannot speculate. This is particularly troublesome when media representatives are outside the door clamoring for a story.

b. Reporters, editors, newscasters. These folks take their job to provide the public *all* the information very seriously. They believe themselves to be acting on behalf of the community. It is a calling. Their line is "Our job is to get the story, no matter what it takes." This is particularly difficult at the beginning of a critical incident when *no one* has the whole story and when most everything that can be said is speculation. Reporters are by nature skeptical and are quick to accuse organizations of stonewalling. Their skepticism is not without foundation, but in the early hours of an event, it is provocative and sometimes difficult to manage.

c. Victims and next of kin. These are the people who are the most affected, the most traumatized, and the most in need of our help and support. Like the rest of us, each of them will internalize and manage their trauma in different ways. Some of them will be the quickest to anger. Some of them will be the first to ask, "Who's to blame?" Again, in those first days when the leaders are struggling themselves to manage the crisis, these sharp, and often poignant words, are hard to hear.

d. The lawyers. Staff lawyers are there from the start to protect the organization from making huge management and communication blunders that leave the organization vulnerable to lawsuits. Perhaps in a corporate lawyer's perfect world, no one would ever say anything about anything. ("Never look your lawyer in the eye," joked one official at the Blacksburg conference, meaning that occasionally you must skip the permission and ask only for forgiveness.) Fortunately, in educational institutions, many lawyers understand that schools are here to care for people, not raise barriers. They are willing to create room to maneuver between the goals of legal perfection and effective communication. Lawyers are very valuable resources.

e. The spokespeople. Whether that is you or your first lieutenant or a member of your communications team, this person is the one who must meld all these refrains into one piece of music. This person has lines such as "This is all we can confirm" and "That information cannot be released because it is part of an ongoing investigation" and "Because of FERPA regulations, I cannot speak to that issue." Hopefully, along the way, that person will also be able to say "Here is the timeline of yesterday's events as we know it today" and "I want to present to you three experts who can answer your questions more thoroughly" and "Tomorrow morning, we will have a list of all the damage with estimates of the cost." The spokesperson always stands on a fault line. It is another balancing act.

- *Someone will sue.* This sad fact is important to acknowledge so that when a suit is filed, its effects are not devastating to everyone's morale. "In our world today, we have a process, a vocabulary, and an expectation that there will always be "a final answer" and probably some kind of remuneration," someone pointed out. "Somehow, we feel we always have to use that process." A suit is another event that calls for leadership.

- *Your organization will always be associated with the tragedy.* Perhaps the folks at Columbine were the first (school people, at least) to articulate this axiom. But it is true. You will always be "the school where the boy was shot" or "the school system where the student drowned" or "the community where the school burned down." Part of that is the news value (however negative) of a brand and part is the residual trauma that lives in peoples' souls that gets revived when your school or district's name is mentioned. There is not much to do about it, but to understand that it is there and that this moment has become part of your organizational landscape.

- *There are always unanticipated blessings.* These can also come under the heading of surprises, but good surprises. The first is that you will get help when you need it. Crisis brings out the best in people. People will just show up at your door, roll up their sleeves, and go to work for you. They will provide help you didn't even know you needed. At Virginia Tech, one gift is the new school spirit and the cohesiveness that has developed among everyone on campus—and, according to the mayor—between the campus and the town as well. There is a genuine warmth and respect among the people there. Even the local media representative and the school administration are saying nice things about each other!

THE MORE THINGS CHANGE

The stories we heard at the seminar that day clearly showed that some pieces of this incident are very new and have radically changed the crisis communication landscape. The key ingredient in these changes is the new technologies we all have at our disposal. These tiny bits and bytes are forcing us into huge adaptations.

- *The ways the data is gathered to report the story have changed.* On the morning of April 16, journalism Professor Roland Lazenby was teaching a class of students in Norris Hall. "My students were no longer novices," he told us. "We had been together for nearly a full year, and they had developed their skills. Some of them had come to Tech having been on their high school newspaper staff. There was a lot of experience in that classroom."

  Norris Hall went into lockdown as the shootings took place. Professor Lazenby barricaded the classroom door, moved the students away from the windows, and put everyone on the floor. The lockdown lasted a long time.

  "To distract the students, I tried to keep lecturing, but I could tell that wasn't working." Somehow, the group decided to begin reporting the story. With cell phones and laptops, the students went to work inside their locked classroom.

  From the university website one student was able to get a roster of the classes in Norris Hall that day. Using university resources and social media websites like Facebook and MySpace, they began to assemble a list of students who were probably in the building—and those students' e-mail addresses and phone numbers. They began trying to contact the students and their friends—mostly by text message. And then they began to write.

  They filed their stories with the webmaster of their class website. He was locked down in another building, but with his laptop at hand he could receive and post the stories to the Web. Soon after the shooting stopped at Norris Hall, students had begun reporting their own stories and eyewitness accounts. Elsewhere on the campus students at the *Collegiate Times* offices, the college newspaper, began posting on their website as well—all with an immediacy and access to sources that made the conventional media envious.

One student outside Norris Hall that day took video of the building with a sound track of the shots. That video instantly made national television. And the most stunning use of the new technology came from the shooter himself, who with camera and computer was able to create his own story, which national television chose to air.

- *How information is disseminated and the story is reported has changed as well.* After the first shootings in the dormitory that morning, the university sent a mass e-mail warning to all students and staff. Probably, on April 16, Tech was well ahead of the national curve among universities in its ability to reach so many people so quickly. Certainly, it was well ahead of many K–12 schools and school districts. Such push e-mail software was only coming into its own in schools. But, as some measure of how fast this technology game is changing, on April 16, 2007, e-mail had already become an antiquated communication system among eighteen- to twenty-two-year-olds. By then, it was all about text messaging. Text messages were what the students were reading. That's why some of them didn't get the warnings.

  As the conventional media reported the story, technology took hold in different ways. Television outlets were looking for stories and pictures to fill a twenty-four-hour news cycle. (Most television stations advertise an address on their home page where anyone can send their digital video, anytime. The definition of "man-on-the-street interview" has stretched to become almost a universal art.) Radio reporters traveled with microphones and tape recorders looking for sound. (They too run twenty-four hours a day.) And the print media was in the 24/7 race, as well, because they not only printed their stories, they posted them to their websites.

  The impact of this real-time media turned this story on its head. Today, once a sound bite takes hold, it reverberates endlessly. Everything is magnified. At Virginia Tech, students and staff alike found themselves pleading with networks and newspapers to take down the disturbing pictures of the shooter, running for the second and third days.

- *A new media has joined the discussion.* Just as Professor Lazenby's students began reporting events to the world without the benefit of a local newspaper or television station, just about anyone, anywhere, who was interested could tell a story about Virginia Tech to anyone else who would listen (or read)—whether or not he or she had any knowledge of the situation.

Facebook, MySpace, and blogs—the social media, as it is called—allow the story to come from an unlimited number of sources, sources that have not been vetted and are not necessarily accurate. In many ways our world is a better place because we all have access to information and can spread information beyond the boundaries set by conventional means. (The pictures of the Buddhist monks protesting in the face of military armor in Myanmar that came out through the Internet is a good example.) But at the same time, this new world puts even greater responsibility on organizations, and on the news media, to get it right and to call attention to the people who have it wrong.

For the most part, on a good day, television and print reporters check their sources. We rely on them to do that. But rumors abound and now spread worldwide at the speed of light. Anyone can say anything on the Web—and it is sometimes difficult to separate truth from fiction. This new media may become our biggest communication challenge.

- *Speed, accessibility, and instant connectivity.* The speed with which communication occurred at Virginia Tech that day was a quantum leap from the day of Columbine. The speed with which details—accurate or not—reached the world was blinding. It changed the way the authorities responded, even as it happened. It has changed the way we will all respond in the future.

Several weeks later, there was a similar, though thankfully smaller, student incident at Delaware State University. Having watched the events at Virginia Tech, the Delaware officials had already installed a text messaging alert system. They notified their student community within thirty-two minutes. That timing has now become the gold standard, though that record will probably not stand long. Several months later, raging brush fires in Southern California caused Pepperdine University to evacuate their students. Newscaster Lester Holt, parent of one of the students, was able to play the university's voice message alert to students and staff from his cell phone on the evening news.

Don't think people aren't watching us. The call to us to be prepared is clear. We have much to learn from our colleagues who have traveled the way.

• • •

State-of-the-art crisis communication—like other kinds of communication—is an ever-changing art, being driven by changes in technology and in stakeholder expectation. In crisis, the stakes are high. The community is watching and lives could be in the balance.

For reflection

1. What can you and your school/district learn from critical incidents in other schools?
2. How can you take advantage of these lessons to better prepare for a critical incident?

NOTE

1. On the morning of April 16, 2007, a Virginia Tech student, shot and killed thirty-two students and faculty members, and wounded many more, in two incidents: the first in a dormitory, the second in Norris Hall, a building of classrooms and science labs. He then took his own life. The incident garnered international media attention.

THE TOOLBOX

17

OVERHAUL DAILY COMMUNICATION

Creating a Collaborative Culture

The newest computer can merely compound, at speed, the oldest problem in the relations between human beings, and in the end the communicator will be confronted with the old problem, of what to say and how to say it.

—Edward R. Murrow

When she started as principal of a small elementary school in the heart of suburbia, Carole didn't expect to be shouted at, cut off, talked down to, and reported to the superintendent—all by folks in her own school community. But by June of her first year at the helm, that's what had happened. Stunned, disheartened, and popping antacids, Carole was told by her boss to turn things around or pack her bags.

Hired because of her reputation as an instructional guru, Carole had an advanced degree in curriculum development and proven success as a teacher. The principal selection committee believed these experiences would be a good match for their community. But a few months into the school year, the community thought otherwise. Described as distant and aloof by parents, Carole was accused by staff members of playing favorites, misunderstanding concerns, and staying in her office with the door closed. Carole's lack of people skills (aka daily communication skills) was undermining her ability to address student achievement.

Later, a member of the selection committee reported that during the panel interview he sensed that Carole was "reserved," and "a little stand-off-ish," but that he and other committee members believed her intellectual grasp of instructional issues would win folks over. Things didn't work that way.

THE LIMITATIONS OF COGNITIVE COMMUNICATION

Carole's communication style was cognitive, intellectual, and formal. This style rests on three assumptions:

- You are working with an audience that has time and will listen to authority.
- Your audience will commit to action without input and is responsive to top-down management.
- Your audience checks their emotional brains at the schoolhouse door, putting aside such needs as the desire for relationships and security.

Carole's style may have gone unchallenged in schools of yesterday when logic held sway. But today's environment requires a different leadership, one built through a daily communication style that fosters connections. Previous assumptions have been turned on their head:

- Audiences are no longer willing to pay attention for very long. Count the number of scene shifts in a fifteen-second TV commercial to understand how minds have been conditioned to be constantly stimulated. Don't like what you're hearing or seeing? Change the channel.
- Top-down leadership lacks power to connect in a world equalized by technology, populated by latch-key children, and shaped by a model of customer service that rewards the squeaky wheel. Two-way communication is a must.
- Emotions are the tollgate the leader must pass through to connect with an audience. Effective communication addresses the human side and answers the practical "what's in it for me?" question.

THE LADDER TO EFFECTIVE DAILY COMMUNICATION

Build Relationships

Relationship development is no longer a soft skill, a luxury or simply something nice to have. Case histories repeatedly show that a sense of community is essential for long-term survival in the work environment. Successful leaders orchestrate a workplace that is connected. They take casual contact seriously and make the effort to speak to people face-to-face. They allow their humanity to show.

Relationships start with knowing people's names. A teacher at one large high school told of a staff picture display in the school's foyer that matched names with faces. She said it was a valuable tool people consulted frequently to learn names of coworkers. "Oh, that's who that is."

When the yearbook teacher, the provider of the display, left the school, the pictures stopped. School leaders failed to notice the staff's disappointment. We asked a teacher why no one said anything. "We thought the principal was too busy taking care of other things," she said, adding, "I'm not sure he even knows my name."

On the other side of this equation, we know of a superintendent in a small school district who shakes the hand of each staff member at the beginning and the end of the school year. And rather than asking staff members to come to him, he goes to them. Walking the hallways, moving in and out of classrooms, pressing flesh, he makes a point of calling staff members by name. And if he doesn't know a name, he asks.

To develop this discipline yourself, consider the following suggestions from fellow practitioners:

- Commit to regular communication.
- Act on your intention.
- Know yourself and be real.
- Listen and learn.
- Change if need be.
- Make yourself available.
- Find the real person in the other.
- Don't let others be wrong.
- Identify and promote strengths.
- Make it clear that your goal is the success of other people.

The Vision Thing

A principal told us recently how surprised—and disappointed—she was to discover that the communication tool least valued by her staff was the school's vision statement. A staff survey showed that countless hours and a wide cross section of community input to express the school's very reason for being seemed to do little to inspire staff behavior.

The principal concluded that writing a vision statement is one thing, that communicating it is quite another matter. Making a school's vision come alive requires the same deliberative planning that goes into writing down the school's underlying belief. Here are some ways to put your vision statement on the lips of all those you wish to follow it.

- Symbolism. Time and money are powerful symbols of what we value. Finding and lavishing both to energetically communicate your school's vision spreads the message to staff and the public that, yes, vision matters. Well-crafted language displayed with attention to color, fonts, and layout are key first steps. Then, decide on strategic placement—from the Web to the newsletter to the classroom.
- Connect the dots. Vision statements are, well, visionary; they're intentionally grand, and intended to set the course for change. But, staff and parents live in the real world where practical blurs big picture. Put communication procedures in place to take notice of small actions that clearly connect to the long-term goal. Then praise individual and collective efforts and results for all to see.
- Who do they think you are? Leaders who live the vision send the most compelling message about its importance. Those who sit behind a closed office door, have an inflexible schedule, or rule by decree send a powerful message about how the school is run. In turn, active listening, focused actions and laughing at yourself send a message that may more closely align with the school's vision. Don't be afraid to show people who you are, what you believe, and that you are also a learner.

Create Opportunities for Dialogue

Listening, truly listening is the secret to genuine two-way communication. How often we hear praise lavished on an administrator for "simply listening" to someone and then repeating back what they heard.

Kowalski, Petersen, and Fusarelli (2007) tell us that people often over-estimate the quality of their listening skills, usually because they define listening narrowly as "hearing." They advise a three-step approach when engaged in conversations.

- Paraphrasing the speaker's comments enables the leader to provide immediate feedback. "So, . . ."
- Perception checking clarifies understanding of the message usually by asking questions. "Is the real problem . . . ?"
- Empathizing with the speaker and being supportive are interpreted as effective listening. "I understand why. . . ." (p. 203)

A high school principal we know credits listening skills for the smooth transition his school community made to a new scheduling model. He engaged the entire community from the start of the discussion and gave equal air to both those who agreed and disagreed. He asked questions. He listened, truly listened, to answers. Everyone knew they were heard and when the change was decided, even those who disagreed were sup-portive.

Build a capacity for listening by shifting the focus from yourself to un-derstanding the experience and point of view of the other person. Do-ing so will impact your emotions, gestures, body language and tone of voice. By simply using the word "you" and considering the thoughts and feelings of your listeners, you'll be more effective.

Jay, a successful school principal works to build that capacity in his school community. "The way a principal can have impact," he says. "is to allow people to be heard. There's no greater tool to build communica-tion than to allow people to have ownership."

One of Jay's first actions when he began work at a new school was an investment in listening; he scheduled a meeting with each member of his fifty-person staff. In conversations of fifteen to thirty minutes, he lis-tened as each staff member talked about school—and home—and what their hopes and dreams were for the upcoming school year. He multi-plied the value of this effort by the attention he gave to the details:

- He sent personalized invitations.
- He found out a little about each staff member before the meeting.
- He allowed no interruptions during the meeting.

- He managed time expectations, but intimated no sense of rush.
- He understood the need for conversation, not judgment.
- He kept the conversation positive.
- He closed the loop with a brief personal e-mail following the meeting.

The dedication of this time to listening was a first step to build employee commitment to their new leader.

Build Tools to Connect

School leaders have lots of information to communicate. Yet, most stakeholders don't have any desire and can't be compelled to slog through mountains of information. What's a leader to do? Streamline messages and make them available to audiences segmented by need to know (e.g., ninth-grade parents, field trip volunteers, and beautification committee members). Here are some other considerations:

- Make access to school information easy and available when and if it is needed. The Web is a perfect tool for self-service information gathering.
- Make a distinction between messages that are "call to action" as opposed to those that are "informational." Color-coding paper to show the difference is a smart idea
- Clarify expressions you use in painting your vision. What do you mean when you say, "We'll do whatever it takes," or "Children are our most precious assets"? Give examples.
- Be precise in your definitions. Some leaders are reluctant to do so for fear of sounding as though they're talking down to audiences. If vertical teaming is an initiative you're pushing, for example, explain exactly how you define it and how it plays out for staff and students.

THROWING NEWSLETTERS AT THE PROBLEM

It's tempting for a leader who's confronted with "a communication breakdown," to create a new communication brochure or another handout. Instead, communication gaps are more effectively addressed by evaluating the quality of relationships built through daily communication. How well do people get along, trust each other, and ask questions?

After a particularly nasty meeting with a parent advisory group, one superintendent came to us. Upset that people didn't seem to appreciate all that was going on in areas of school improvement, the superintendent suggested publishing a newsletter would solve the problem. We asked some questions:

- What were the parents saying?
- What were the sources of the friction points?
- Where were people getting their information?
- Would a newsletter close the communication gap?

His own answers persuaded him to rethink what was really going on.

The superintendent put the newsletter idea aside and instead focused his efforts on establishing a pattern of intentional communication aligning his beliefs about education with existing tools. He crafted precise messages that communicated the value he placed on bringing the community together to address the needs of children. He arrived early for meetings and spent time in informal conversation and intentional listening. He closed communication loops after meetings by following up with personal responses to questions and concerns.

For each meeting he planned three big messages with language and examples that people could view as take-away messages. He repurposed these messages by using them in other venues such as the district newsletter, website, and meetings with staff. Several months of this approach helped him create the kind of relationships that a multipage newsletter could never have achieved.

• • •

A pattern of consistent messages delivered through multiple means in daily communication is the leader's bread and butter. Connections with the community that are real and spontaneous, rather than staged, lead to active participation and engagement in a culture where being right is not the point, but being heard is. This happens through planning, diligence, and commitment. The leader who does this will succeed.

For reflection

1. What communication techniques are used in your school/district to promote relationships?
2. What can you do to evaluate the effectiveness of your daily communication with staff and community?
3. Are the daily communication tools you have in place serving your leadership goals? How?

READ YOUR SCHOOL (OR DISTRICT) NEWSLETTER

Understanding Why Parents Don't

My words fly up, my thoughts remain below.
Words without thoughts never to heaven go.

—William Shakespeare

If a school newsletter is as American as apple pie, then why do so few parents embrace it as a signature connection to their child's education? Sure, PTA officers swear they read it, an occasional parent may comment on an article, and many parents intend to read it—later. But, how shall we put this gently? Most parents just don't give the newsletter the attention we would like.

Filled with possibilities for connecting in significant ways, most school newsletters we've evaluated simply don't. We know this is painful to hear, especially when you've put time and talent, heart and soul into this regular publication. The sad fact is that heart and soul alone are not enough to keep your message out of the trash and move it onto the refrigerator door.

YOUR BULLY PULPIT

A school newsletter that parents don't read is a failure. Effective leaders view the newsletter as a working asset, an opportunity to influence positive interactions between families and school. Yet, some newsletter practices fail families. Simply publishing four or five pages without responding to the significant communication barriers that often exist between schools and communities—length and time, lack of relevance or real authenticity—is wasted effort.

We believe a school or district newsletter becomes a great communication asset when *its mission is to anticipate reader's needs and expectations.* The successful leader's newsletter *influences* parents to *participate* in an event, *understand* the vagaries of the school's testing program, *appreciate* the value of arts education. To influence an audience, the school leader must see the newsletter as a way to *build relationships.* Minus relationships, you have no influence. Without influence, you can't be a successful leader.

A RELATIONSHIP BUILDING TOOL

Consider the current state of your relationship with the parents in your school or district. Since all relationships are built from the ground up, consider your newsletter the paper equivalent of a firm handshake. It tells readers who you are. Through pictures and words, the newsletter offers readers an opportunity to take the school's measure. Yep, that's what readers do when they look at your newsletter—draw conclusions about you and your school.

Thinking about the publication in that way might make you pause over these school newsletter headlines:

- Gift Wrap Sale a Success
- Happy Holidays
- Three More Months 'til Summer Vacation

Each, in a different way, undermines that leader's influence by telegraphing to the reader these values: selling stuff, celebrating the holidays, and marking time before the school year ends. Certainly, these values are not what any school leader intends to communicate.

BE RELEVANT

A key element in a successful school or district newsletter, one that parents read, is relevance. Making a newsletter, or any piece of communication for that matter, relevant means dealing with real issues and touching the hearts of those you want to influence. Learning *why* readers are interested and *what* they perceive as the value of reading are first steps.

Terry is a principal who asked for our help in redesigning her twelve-page monthly newsletter. She started by describing her community as "expecting a lot of detailed information from the school. They look forward to the newsletter as a way to keep up with what's going on here."

Time and further study revealed a different truth. We met with some of her school's parents in a focus group and discovered the dirty truth: they weren't reading the newsletter. This was a tough thing for Terry to hear, yet with further thought, she realized that newsletters from her own son's school sat unread on her nightstand. It happens to the best of us.

We met with other parents in her school to find out how they determined relevance in the newsletter and whether they saw the newsletter as a valuable link to the school. (We've since met with many other parents and asked the same questions.) We armed them with red pens and promises of anonymity and asked them to review their children's school newsletter. Our instructions were to mark an x over things they wouldn't read and draw a circle around those they would. Big red x's outnumbered circles by a wide margin. That's humbling even for the most confident school leader.

It doesn't take the parents long to describe what they find relevant and prescribe a cure for ailing newsletters. Here, in brief, is what they say:

Start with a Calendar

Over and over, parents have told us this is the most important tool for information delivery. And they want "a calendar that looks like a calendar," a monthly or biweekly view. Parents say if they don't look at anything else, they've read the calendar.

Let Them Skim

We're a nation of skimmers and scanners, glancing through newsletter headlines for something relevant as we stand poised next to a wastebasket, ready to clear out paper that is not useful. Estimates suggest that the average American will give you just three to five seconds to make your case.

Your goal is to make it easy for readers to locate the information they want and need. You do that through headlines. Writing headlines requires a focus on what you want the reader to know or do as a result of reading further. Your motivations might include wanting parents to learn about a new school program, take action to help their own child, or support the school's tutoring program. Table 18.1 shows some examples of headlines revised to impact the reader.

Prioritize Information

A parent described her frustration in reading the newsletter this way: "I can't decide what's important to read. You give the same attention to the school fun fair as you do to school test scores." Her indictment reflects the need for thoughtful planning of newsletter content.

Establish regular column headings to help organize your content. Categories might include: information you must know, what happened last month (briefly), what's happening next month. Be sparing in the amount of information you include in each column, and position them in the same place in each issue of the newsletter. Lead with your most important story. This helps both you and your reader.

Make Information Concise

Use bullets, graphics, pictures. A *USA Today* approach of short articles, bullet information, graphics, and pictures makes information delivery more effective. Less is more. A brief summary of information is ef-

Table 18.1.   Revised Headlines

Before	After
New Teacher Program	Noontime Web Video Revitalizes Lunch at Desk
Ways to Help Your Child	Helping with Homework 101: How to Get Started
PTA Seeks Volunteers for Tutoring	The Case of the Missing Volunteer

fective for newsletter readers. If needed, make more lengthy descriptions available on the school website.

Rewrite the Principal's or Superintendent's Message

Today's parents expect to be engaged and addressed in language they understand. Keep your message brief, timely. Don't use jargon, long sentences or paragraphs. Avoid approaching topics from a philosophical bent (see chapter 19).

Two-Way Communication

One way to communicate your authenticity is to solicit your readers' comments. Even though their comments may make you wince, encourage them and pay attention to them. It adds authenticity to your publication and will turn it into a "must read."

One of the best school newsletters we've seen is one in which the principal took comments from a school suggestion box and answered them in each edition. Suggestions included questions about school lavatories and the sixth-grade math program; complaints about the timing of parent events and the amount of homework. She always kept her answers short and friendly. Often the question and answer exchange resulted in action and change.

The time and risk she took in preparing this column paid off in increased reader loyalty and in her audience's increased understanding of the obstacles she faced in leading the school. She showed an openness to dialogue with her community. Parents and staff commented often on her column. It became a springboard for healthy discussion and turned her newsletter into an influential communication tool.

● ● ●

Creating sensible, achievable goals for your newsletter allows you to work from a position of strength and to create a broad coalition of constituents. While websites and e-mail bring speed and efficiency to our communication, brief print newsletters (also put them online) can continue to play a role.

The very act of creating strong relationship-building messages makes people better leaders. It requires first doing the intellectual work of figuring out what our point of view is and then the creative work of putting that point of view into a form that makes it accessible and interesting to others.

The school newsletter has the potential to be a strong force in shaping parent views. The chance to inspire positive action is in your hands. The collaborative relationships that result from a thoughtful publication improve interactions between home and school.

Readers regularly build relationships and loyalties with favorite magazines, newspaper columnists, authors. They look for authenticity, humor, intelligence, inspiration, and perspective. Parents approach the school newsletter with the same expectations. Don't disappoint them.

For reflection

1. Test your newsletter by giving it to a trusted parent and asking him or her to look at it for ten seconds and tell you what it said and what the call to action was. If they can't tell you, how would you revise?
2. Ask your front office staff to name the five most common questions parents ask. How are these questions addressed in the school newsletter?
3. Apply the red pen test to a school newsletter. Cross out what you wouldn't read, circle what you would. Describe common elements of the cross-outs and the circles.

(19)

MANAGE YOUR SCHOOL (OR DISTRICT) WEBSITE

Ensuring This Powerful Tool Works for You

No man is an island.

—John Donne

In a shrinking world, it's sometimes easier to get information about what's happening on the banks of the Amazon than it is to find out what time your child's school is dismissing in a snowstorm. The challenge for school leaders is clear: move to the Web.

Think of the school or district website as an ATM machine, a self-service checkout line or an E-Z Pass on a car windshield. From the user's point of view, each is all about convenience. Users avoid lines, whiz through tollbooths, and become self-sufficient at accomplishing routine tasks. Parents and the community demand the same easy info-highway to their schools.

A school or district that offers at its website self-service information, a place to do business easily, and an invitation for interaction will brand itself as a go-to organization that values its community. Done right, that website is a smart political tool that connects with audiences. Think of a pajama-clad, Gen Xer working mom at midnight downloading a misplaced permission slip for her fifth grader's field trip. Before long, it's printed, signed, and tucked in the backpack. Think of the dad who couldn't attend a school event, but who can look at photos of student work at his computer and post supportive comments to the class. These are two happy customers. Chalk two up for the school.

A STRATEGIC COMMUNICATION TOOL

The Web is the place to do business, build a reputation, and make friends. Once you've established your website as the go-to resource for essential school information, you will be able to use it as a key strategic communication tool. For example, you can use it to tame the school grapevine. Communities abuzz, particularly about controversial issues, can often be cooled with accurate information offered quickly and updated frequently. A smart leader will deploy the Web to make this happen.

Keep your ear to the ground. What is your network telling you about the community mood? Those who answer your office phones, supervise street crossings, or take tickets at football games are in a unique position to have the inside scoop. People often talk more openly to these folks than they would with a school administrator. Listen to what they are saying. Then, use the Web as a quick way to control rumors (not necessarily all of them, use your judgment) with relevant information.

The Web would have helped one school community manage a communication gap that turned ugly. Here's what happened:

The school notified parents in the spring that at the start of the next school year, their sixth graders would move to a new school. They would transfer from the elementary to a secondary building for grades six to twelve. Parents were supportive of the decision and students were excited about the move. But when spring turned to summer with no further communication from the school, parents started to get anxious.

It began in June with sideline discussions at Little League games. By July, parents were anxiously calling the school for information. They wanted to know what plans were being made and how to prepare their child for the transition to the new school. What would the schedule look like? Who were the teachers? Would they be mixed in with the high school kids? In the parents' view, response from the school ranged from none to hostile.

School leaders had turned their focus inward and were dealing with complications in the building renovation project and the sudden resig-

nation of the guidance department chairperson. Because of these pressing demands, administrators believed they could put off communication
with parents until the week before school opened when they would give
them complete information.

Parents didn't see it this way. They viewed the lack of communication
as evidence that "no one at the school knew anything." By August, they
were not only questioning the administrators' ability to plan, but the wisdom of moving the sixth graders in the first place. They wondered if
their children wouldn't be better off just staying in the "safety" of the elementary building. Parents' initial acceptance and excitement about the
move had turned to antagonism and hostility.

While school administrators were acting in good faith, their miscalcu-
lation of the community's need for updated information resulted in a
communication vacuum. Assumptions by the school—that parents
trusted the school and were willing to wait, that parents were on vacation, that August would be plenty of time to get them information—
were all incorrect. Communication vacuums are always filled with misinformation, rumors, and judgments. Anger sets in, sparking power
struggles.

The vacuum could have been filled efficiently by the school website,
using it as an up-to-date communication tool. Imagine if just these small
bits of information had been posted and updated all summer:

- A timeline for the move including a date for sixth-grade orientation
- A school supply list for students
- A construction update with pictures of the progress
- Coming soon: a profile of our new guidance director
- An announcement of the information that would be shared with
  parents, including how it will be sent and when

Posting this information would have likely taken less staff time than answering the calls that came to the school office about this issue. Certainly, this approach would have prevented the significant damage done
to the parent-school relationship.

Using the Web as a mouthpiece establishes leadership and gives you
the platform to get accurate information to your parents. Establishing
these communication channels and providing a steady stream of information *before* there's a communication crisis will serve you well. Failure

to take the information reins may result in others seizing control. We've seen it happen over and over.

Resource: E School News
http://www.eschoolnews.com/
Check out this resource for all things related to school technology. A regular feature, Site of the Week, points to effective school Web practices on a variety of topics, including using the Web for school communication and collaboration.

PROVIDE ESSENTIAL INFORMATION

From the user's perspective, the core of a self-service website is knowledge acquisition and speed. On a well-designed site, user needs trump mission statements, jargon-ridden discourse, and razzle-dazzle. A website that strives to impress without addressing basic user needs hasn't done its job. User-centered design avoids deadly mistakes like these:

- Lack of contact information, address or telephone number
- A page that is slow to load because of too many graphics and gizmos
- Long paragraphs of nonactionable information
- Sadly out-of-date material; lack of freshly updated news
- Pictures and images that are not relevant to the core audience
- Site navigation focused on organizational structure and wording, and not intuitive to users

Web visitors who are confused and frustrated never get past the home page. A successful site focuses on the users—it answers their questions, anticipates their needs, and offers them opportunities to be a contributing member of the school community.

Start planning, or updating, your school website by identifying your users. They will include parents, prospective parents, elected officials, real estate agents, media, and members of the school community. Find out what each of the groups wants and needs to know about your school. You can collect this information through informal written surveys, by gathering questions routinely handled by front-office staff or by including this topic as an agenda item when you meet with various groups

One principal collected that input in developing a Web page for the parents of new kindergarteners. She invited several parents and some teachers to her office and led a discussion about the hopes and fears surrounding that milestone year in a child's and parent's life. What information would help them get through this time?

Following that conversation, the principal and a school team used parent input to identify information and designed an award-winning Web page packed with content that engaged parents and involved their children. It included details on a typical day in kindergarten, pictures and profiles of kindergarten teachers, the new things kindergarteners learn, and reasons why school is so much fun. Parents were able to download required forms and note important dates. They came to the orientation event enthusiastic and with a positive feeling about the school. Without ever having stepped inside the school, they had developed a relationship with the staff. The Web can do this.

The Eyes Have It

Here are some tips that take advantage of readers' eye movement as they look at Web pages:

- Text attracts attention before graphics. Contrary to prevailing thought, images are not the first thing readers look at on a website. Most users come to your site for information—plain old text.
- Users look at the top left before moving down and to the right. People generally scan Web pages in the shape of an *F*—so make sure the important elements of your content are located in these key areas.
- When it comes to type size, smaller may be better. Smaller fonts appear to increase focused viewing while larger fonts encourage scanning.
- Shorter paragraphs and sentences work better than long ones. The fleeting attention span of Internet users is no myth. Write accordingly.
- One-column formats perform better than multicolumn. Much of the information contained in multiple columns will be ignored because readers feel overwhelmed. Simpler really is better.
- White space is good. Fight the temptation to fill up your Web page. Users will ignore portions of your content when there's too much going on. Allow some visual open space for readers to rest their eyes. (Laun, 2007)

MAKE INFORMATION EASY TO FIND

Readers' needs are as nuanced as paint chips at Home Depot. That doesn't mean you have to offer the Web equivalent of seventeen shades of red, but you do have to offer alternatives for those who only want the quick take versus those who want all the details.

One way to do this is by organizing your messages into segments. Marilynne Rudick and Leslie O'Flahavan, E-WRITE partners and authors of *Clear, Correct, Concise E-Mail: A Writing Workbook for Customer Service Agents* (2002), suggest thinking of the segments as a bite, snack, and meal. The bite is the headline. Using a subject and a verb, a bite telegraphs the message and gives the reader a decision point from which he can decide if he wants or needs to go further. Additional information is in the snack, a few targeted sentences that summarize the high points. The meal is the everything-you-wanted-to-know-and-more about the topic. Because most readers' interests are satisfied with the bite and snack, those two components of the message should stand together, with a link to the meal.

- Bite: School dismisses at noon on November 15.
- Snack: Students will be dismissed at noon on Friday, November 15. A national expert in math instruction is providing a three-hour program for all staff during the afternoon.
- Meal: Biography of the national expert, link to the expert's website, link to an article about the expert or a document illustrating the concepts that your teachers will learn.

CONSISTENCY IS KEY

Like other great American frontiers, the Web was first populated by homesteaders and cowboys who liked to do things their own way. But today, because consistency is central to a successful website, school staff members need to put aside a desire to do their own thing. Web users have little patience for creative differences in navigation and style as they move from page to page.

A Webmaster needs support from the whole school team to provide content and technical expertise, but the piecemeal approach of many cooks (staff members) with varying principles and random rationales posting material at will spoils the stew. While involvement of all staff should be encouraged, a single Web leader needs to have responsibility for pulling it all together. Strict adherence to a common vision, elements, symbols, and navigation system makes the user's visit seamless and focuses attention where it belongs: on the content

Technical ability is critical to creating a successful site, but it's not the only key. The kind of person who seems to work best as the Webmaster is someone who is also

- Skilled at listening and addressing the needs of the end user
- Skilled at writing and organizing information for clarity
- Able to exercise control over Web content and effectively translate the needs of school and parent leaders without simply abdicating to their demands

WORK SMART

With your support and direction, your webmaster can find plenty of shortcuts and money-saving options for your website that will not compromise the quality of the site.

- Leverage resources: link to content about curriculum, policies, and so on elsewhere on the site, instead of re-creating them.
- Send your Webmaster for training offered others—the state, associations, community colleges.
- Use other school sites as models. (The National School Public Relations Association annually posts the names and URLs of award-winning school and district sites.)
- Make use of free or inexpensive tools or services from other sources, such as search tools, survey tools, hosting and content management, video and photo sharing, newsletters, and list management.

ONE WORD OF CAUTION

The website is something the leadership—not parents, students, or volunteers—must own. The site is as important as any another resource
available to the leader. Parents don't write lesson plans, they don't hire
staff, and they should not control the communication through the Web.
Nightmares abound of the consequences of parents or students given
this responsibility.

- A high school webmaster graduates, then swaps out all of the administrators' photos with Seinfield characters. No one knew how to
  change it back.
- A parent webmaster "graduates" from elementary to middle
  school. The school leader is left to start the website from scratch
  with a new group of volunteers.
- A growing number of parents are organizing "official" and "unoffi-
  cial" e-mail lists for school communities, but who owns the lists and
  who is responsible for moderating (or not moderating) the content
  for accuracy and possible legal implications?

In one community, a middle school parent compiled her own listserv
of parent names and e-mails. She organized the list under the guise of
supporting the school, but it quickly morphed into a vehicle for personal
attacks and misinformation. Lack of a school information alternative led
many unwary parents to sign up for her list. In retrospect, it's easy to see
that leadership could have prevented, or certainly mitigated, this mess
by preemptive action of their own to connect parents and communicate
with them through a school-sponsored list serve.

A BRAVE NEW WORLD

The message is this: take the bull by the horns and make your website
(and accompanying social media tools—see next chapter) the go-to
place for trusted, up-to-date information. As leader, your investment of
time and resources into this rich and ever-expanding tool will speak to
parents who have grown up in a technology-enriched world in ways that
newsletters, fliers, and memos cannot. The immediacy of the 24/7 con-

nection between home and school has vast potential for uniting schools and their communities in the effort to educate children. Your school's website turns your virtual community into an engaged one.

• • •

The task of building and maintaining a website and e-mail distribution list is complicated. School leadership needs to keep current with the continually changing technology, understand the need for school responsiveness to community, and make the effort to translate complicated information into digestible chunks.

For reflection

1. On a scale of 1–10, rate how your school's website serves the needs of your community. What could be done in the next few months to improve it?
2. Describe a recent incident in your organization when communication was an issue. How would making information available on the Web have served to bridge communication gaps?
3. Define the Web demographics of your community. What percentage of your community would choose to receive school information via the website?

20

GET A GRIP ON SOCIAL MEDIA

Playing a Role in Web Conversation

You just can't afford to ignore what is going on in social media.

—Jill Kurtz

Imagine this: in less than half a second, over 500,000 pieces of information are at your fingertips chronicling every facet of a single incident happening at your school. Want to try? Fire up Google and type in "Jena Six." There you'll find all the information (and disinformation) that's out there about a school confrontation that went national all through the power of the blogosphere.

What started as a group of black students in Jena, Louisiana, asking permission from a school leader to sit under a tree usually occupied by white students, turned into in a series of racially charged incidents that resulted in radically different punishments for the white students and the black students. Initially, most mainstream media ignored the story.

Social media did not. Hundreds of interlinked bloggers told the story of the Jena Six to thousands of readers. Blogs helped raise over $200,000 in legal defense funds for the students. Online petitions were circulated, and over 10,000 supporters rallied in support of the Jena Six.

James Rucker, executive director of the Internet-based civil rights group Color of Change, believes this story took hold in the blogosphere because that medium has no reluctance in tackling thorny issues. The lack of filters and gatekeepers allows for free-flowing discussion.

"At its core, it's citizen journalism," Rucker said. "As a blogger you can communicate easily and rapidly. Social media pushes mainstream media to take notice" (Allen, 2007). Take notice they did, and the national and international mainstream media played catch-up with social media first responders.

CONVERSATION IS HERE TO STAY

Web 2.0 (social media) is here, and it's not going away. It's reshaping the way people interact with each other and their schools. As foreign as it may seem, school leaders need to find ways to harness its power. Schools must not allow themselves to be left behind by a digitally adept public that is moving forward at the speed of light. Such a disconnect will only make leading schools and school districts more difficult.

Let's not freak out. Remember how calm we were about adopting e-mail and the Web? (Oh, wait a minute. We freaked out then, too.) We can do this, just take a deep breath and read on.

In the new world, everyone is a potential publisher. There are no more filters. The power of Google and other search engines makes it easy and quick to find anything. Type in "competent school administrator" and you've got over 200,000 hits (Good news: "incompetent school administrator" only gets 150,000). Add to the power of Google the fact that anyone can make a website, start a blog, post a picture. What you've got is enough to scare the bejeezus out of the most confident school leader.

But look at it another way. Google, social media, and Web 2.0 present a set of tools, tools that offer the ability to reach stakeholders and influence community discussion like never before. Social media can become another way for schools to communicate, like a newsletter, an e-mail or a website.

Steve Hockett, principal in residence at the U.S. Department of Education, Office of Education Technology, is one of the developers of School 2.0 tools to assist districts in planning for schools of tomorrow.

"The flattening of the world demands we bring people into the school. Technology is the platform to make it happen," Hockett says. "Not doing so means giving up a lot of opportunities for engagement."

A SOCIAL MEDIA PRIMER

The words *social media* describe online technologies and practices that people use to share opinions, experiences, and perspectives with each other. Unlike traditional media (television, newspapers, radio, etc.), which are one-way and static, social media thrive on interaction and real-time feedback. Anybody can publish on social media, which are linkable and easily reused.

Some of the most common examples of social media follow:

- Blog. A blog (Web log) is a website where entries are commonly displayed in reverse chronological order, the last on top. *Blog* can also be used as a verb, meaning to maintain or add content to a blog. Many blogs provide commentary or news on a particular subject; others function as more personal online diaries. A typical blog combines text, images, and links to other blogs, Web pages, and other media related to its topic. The ability for readers to leave comments in an interactive format is an important part of many blogs.
- Wiki. A wiki is software that allows users to create, edit, and link Web pages easily. Wiki websites are often also referred to as *wikis*; for example, Wikipedia is considered one of the best known wikis. Wikis are being installed by businesses to provide affordable and effective Intranets and for sharing knowledge and experience.
- Social networking: Online communities (e.g., MySpace, Facebook, LinkedIn) allow people to share interests and activities. Most provide various ways for users to interact, such as chat, messaging, e-mail, video, voice chat, file sharing, blogging, discussion groups, and so on. The content is wide-ranging. You can even watch opera clips on YouTube.
- Video Sharing. YouTube is a video sharing website where users can upload, view, share, and comment on video clips. In addition to being a popular website for users to share video, the service is widely used by bloggers as a video repository.
- Photo Sharing. Flickr is a photo-sharing website. In addition to being a popular website for users to share personal photographs, the service is widely used by bloggers as a photo repository.

All of these websites typically use technologies such as blogs, message boards, and podcasts, to allow users to interact with each other. Their attraction is rooted in sharing common interests, learning new things and making business connections. They also offer opinion and context for information found elsewhere. A parent looking for a new school for her child, may first go to official school websites, but will surely Google school names and check the neighborhood blogs.

A recent study by the Pew Internet and American Life Project (2007) showed that 93 percent of teens use the Internet, and more of them than ever are treating it as a venue for social interaction. Their parents push to catch up and increasingly see the value social networking has for them.

Blogs and social networking sites are no longer just for the young, however. A survey conducted by Ketcham and the University of Southern California Annenberg Strategic Public Relations Center, *Media Myths and Realities: A Public of One* (2008), shows increasing use across age groups of new media.

- Among U.S. fifty-five- to sixty-four-year-olds, 17 percent of consumers reported using blogs this year, compared to just 7 percent in 2006; and 11 percent are using social networking sites, up from 4 percent.
- U.S. consumers fifty-five to sixty-four turn to search engines more than the average consumer, with 72 percent using search in 2007, compared to 54 percent in 2006.
- Among U.S. consumers sixty-five and older, 16 percent are using blogs and 11 percent use social networking sites, compared to 8 percent and 1 percent, respectively, in 2006.
- 65 percent of consumers sixty-five and older use search engines, up from 55 percent.

The need for schools to get on board is clear. To be part of the conversation, leaders need to go where the action is—social media.

A TEACHABLE MOMENT

Nurturing worthwhile ideas provides a powerful alternative to gossip. But if we don't have access to the new tools, we are not even in the discussion, and we look very old-fashioned. The far-reaching effects of these tools are illustrated by the following local incident that recently turned into a national media event.

A student leaves a message on the *home* phone of a school district's chief operating officer, questioning the leader's wisdom in deciding to keep school open during a snowfall in the area. The COO's wife retrieves the message and becomes angry. Very angry. She concludes that the call and message is a violation of her family's privacy. She responds by leaving a harsh message on the student's cell phone. The harsh message angers the student and winds up on YouTube. A very public conversation begins: newspapers, columnists, at least one major editorial, CNN, the evening news, and national morning talk shows.

Everyone—parents, students, politicians, and pundits—had an opinion. Tens of thousands jumped online to listen to the wife's message and join the highly charged conversation. It was swift, visceral, divided. It was very difficult for the COO and his family. It resulted in punishment for the student.

Flare-ups like these are new online versions of the age-old clash between adolescent behavior and authority. One role of school leaders is to turn these flare-ups into teachable moments, in part by using their own social media outlets. For instance, as tempers cool, the school leader might use his or her blog to become part of the online discussion by opening a discussion around questions such as:

- How do we shape the right to privacy in the electronic age?
- What are the responsibilities that come with free-style posting?
- What are future implications for information posted today?
- What about respect for one's elders?
- What core values are important in creating an online presence?

New tools offer new opportunities to do what we do, better. Without them, we not only appear clueless about what's being said, but powerless to impact it. Not every conversation requires a response, but it is crucial that the leader be aware of what's being said, to be able to put it in context and to have the means to join the discussion. The risk of inaction (the new ROI) is great.

Is a community group challenging your new math curriculum? Rather than lurking on the sidelines of the group's online petition and Internet discussion group, champion and establish a dialogue with these stakeholders that is relevant, authentic, and engaging. Establish the context for the decisions.

Test scores, suspension rates, demographics, and other pieces of content are an easy click away—if not on your website, on someone else's. Your parents know how to find them. But, along with information, parents and community members seek context to make informed decisions. What is being done about the teacher who was arrested for child pornography? Why are calculators and not memorization used in teaching math? Why is the school serving vegetarian lunches?

Answers to these questions will be created either by people who are conjecturing or by a school leader who takes charge of the issue and provides a social media platform for addressing the issue in context. We think you will be a lot happier if you take the lead.

MOVE FROM LURKER TO PARTICIPANT

A Texas school system (Clear Creek ISD) makes use of a social media tool on its website to correct disinformation. School leaders encourage stakeholders to e-mail them rumors, which they post and address with correct information. The website also deploys podcasts, video, and pictures as tools to lead the conversation about their schools. Here are some other newly-adopted practices:

- Many systems have moved from blanket e-mails to RSS feeds that allow recipients to pick and choose what they want to hear about.
- Podcasts and streaming video making their way to some school system sites. Fairfax County Public Schools, for example, provides podcasts and video of many community meetings
- Superintendents, principals, and teachers across the nation are creating blogs to connect with community, parents, and students.

To get started in applying social media tools, think about the possibilities outlined below.

Monitoring

Learn about existing blogs that talk about your community and monitor them. There are software tools that will "push" new postings to you via e-mail, so you don't have to go searching. If the bloggers or commenters are talking about your school or an issue you care about, participate in the conversation. This says you are engaged and involved. It says you are willing to talk even when you don't control the conversation. Many parents may assume you are seeing these listings even if you are not, and your lack of response may be saying something unfavorable about you and your school.

Monitoring What People Are Saying
Here are some sites to help you keep track of mentions of your school name:

- Blogpulse.com
- Technorati.com
- Blogsearch.google.com
- Search.blogger.com

LinkedIn

This resource (www.linkedin.com) allows school leaders and staff to post professionally focused bios. It's Facebook for adults. Parents can be invited to link in, giving them a way to reach teachers, and teachers a way to reach parents. It eliminates the need to maintain any off-line contact groups. Leaders could also set up a "group" on this site, and invite parents to join.

RSS Feeds

This tool allows users from your school's home page to register and receive updates on topics of interest to them. Interested in getting news about the football team, but not the baseball team? How about news on senior class activities or the drama club? An RSS feed allows the school leader to make it easy for people to keep up with news on topics unique to their interests.

Blogging Tools

Schools that have little or no budget for technology can turn to blog-ging software as a low-cost or no-cost solution for website content man-agement. Blogging software eliminates the need for technical knowl-edge and offers "widgets" that can enhance functionality with little effort. Most tools include calendars and sign-ups for an e-newsletter. Blogging is a new communication tool for a school leader to interact with the community. Blogging does *not* mean that you must accept com-ments. Comments can be invited, only if you choose. Allowing site visi-tors to post comments means giving up some control of site content, but doing so says very good things about the transparency of your school.

Those in schools who are over forty are all learning together. As fast as we get one new skill under our belt, another new tool appears. It's about attitude: we have to see this as an adventure, not a crushing sen-tence. No matter how daunting it may seem, we have to move forward; if not, we and our schools will be left way behind. The worst thing to do is to say it doesn't matter. It does.

• • •

Social media are firmly entrenched, and the dynamic back and forth shapes public opinion in ways never thought possible. Their power is multiplied with the convergence of blogs, wikis, video, and social net-working, all working in tandem. Add traditional media to the mix, and we've got a whole new way of expression. Used strategically, social me-dia provide the platform school leaders need to develop deeper bonds with their communities.

For reflection

1. Talk with members of your staff about their use of social media. Do teachers use these media as an instructional tool? What is the general level of acceptance of social media as a way to engage stu-dents and community?
2. How comfortable would you be creating a micro blog (small blog) as a way of communicating internally with staff? What are the pos-itive and negative implications of accepting comments?
3. Take note of the style of writing used in blogs. What steps can or should the school take to adapt the social media writing style to ef-forts of their own.

WRITE WITH PURPOSE

Harnessing the Punch of the Written Word

I try to leave out the parts people skip.

—Elmore Leonard

A growling, stormy Sunday night, and Superintendent Edward Norris of Hopeful County Schools slouches in front of a glowing computer screen. The lightning cracks, the family cat screeches, and Dr. Norris almost jumps out of his pajamas. He tries to focus on the dreaded task of writing his message for the district newsletter instead of checking on the game.

There's no raven perched on the door, but this scene is certainly familiar to superintendents, principals, and other administrators, who, too often, file writing that message under must do, mundane, routine. But with parents and the public increasingly pressing their legitimate demand to know what's going on at school and where their tax dollars are going, successful administrators can't do a pro forma job of it anymore. They must connect with energy, command, and respect.

Write well, because there's nothing that makes school staff and parents crumple the newsletter or push the delete button faster than the tired old "Welcome back, folks . . . the French Club will meet on Tuesday this year—and let's have a fine year!" Instead, the written word should shine a light on your forward-looking efforts and light a fire under your very unique clients.

Absent this fire, school writing degenerates into happy talk, philosophical mumbo jumbo or jargon-filled dictums that contribute to community apathy. If you're strong in every other realm of communication, your community may forgive poor written communication. ("He's a great leader, but, man, he can't write," she said, eyes widening.) Otherwise, poor writing may be just one more missed opportunity to rally your community around your vision.

PASS THE "SO WHAT" TEST

Leaders measure effectiveness of writing by asking a simple question: so what? Writing is effective, when it results in outcomes like these:

- The community understands the clear choices you've made in the budget process.
- The staff member is able to explain how the school vision impacts her teaching.
- The parent makes informed decisions about the options for her child's early childhood education.

Each outcome demonstrates that the writing has produced an impact and influenced how the reader thinks and acts.

Writing is an opportunity to build a relationship. Just as we connect with people through speaking conducting formal and informal meetings, walking the hallways before school, standing on the sidelines at a football game—we can relate to our stakeholders through our writing. A column in the newsletter, an agenda for a meeting, a memo to staff—all are occasions to build relationships.

Planning for Writing Success
- Set realistic goals.
- Research readers' needs and address them.
- Seek constant feedback and make changes.
- Turn boring topics into compelling stories.
- Convert abstract school vision into specific action.
- Use real people to illustrate the big picture.
- Infuse your stories with color, voice, and style.

KNOW WHAT YOU WANT TO ACCOMPLISH

How can you as a leader build skills to turn your writing into another means of connecting?

First, by developing clarity around the reason you're writing. Start by breaking down your reasons into usable categories:

- Inform. Tell the news.
- Explain. Tell the hows and whys of ideas and issues.
- Engage. Tell stories and allow and encourage reader comment.
- Entertain. Convey items of human interest and recognition.
- Interpret. Demystify the school experience.

The following example demonstrates what happens when too many reasons are packed into one paragraph:

> Three different approaches to early childhood education are available. At the Happy Valley School, there are two progressive programs serving children, while the Powell School houses a highly regarded Montessori program. All options are available to families who live within the designated boundaries or who apply for out-of-boundary admission.

This "everything but the kitchen sink" approach is confusing. Look at it from a reader's point of view:

- Inform: OK, I get that the school has three different approaches, but does early childhood education mean kindergarten?
- Explain: I guess I have to make a choice, but when, how? How do I know if I live in the designated boundary? How do I apply for out-of-boundary admission? Does early childhood education mean kindergarten?
- Interpret: Progressive programs? Highly regarded Montessori program? What does all that mean? Does early childhood education mean kindergarten?

So, let's go back and reevaluate the early childhood education paragraph by breaking it up into chunks of information, each of which has a different purpose:

- Writing to inform:
  - Bulleted information that tells who (is involved), what (decision needs to be made) and when (the decision must be made)
  - A calendar that lists the steps in the decision process and gives important dates.
  - A website list where parents can go for additional information.
- Writing to explain
  - Bulleted information that explains the how and why. How should parents make a choice? Why is there more than a single program?
  - A map to show the boundary areas.
  - A simplified list of steps to navigate the out-of-boundary admission process.
- Writing to interpret
  - A schedule of open houses when parents can see program options in practice.
  - A description of a typical day in each program.
  - A list of quotes from teachers about each program.
  - A list of quotes from parents of children currently in each program.
- Writing to engage
  - A blog that includes links to all of the above. An invitation to parents to submit questions and comments.

Each of these chunks could be a separate article or Web link—or the chunks could be combined as sections in a longer piece. How you present the material will be determined by your choice of medium.

THINK BEYOND THE PARAGRAPH

Administrators turned writers have plenty of information to get across. To get your arms around disorganized information, think outside the prose box. Paragraphs and sentences of prose are appropriate and effective in some circumstances. For example, if you have a story to tell—something with a beginning, middle, and an end—then write it in paragraphs.

But, today readers are accustomed to *USA Today* style of information delivery. Short stories are accompanied by sidebars designed around such formats as

- Bulleted lists
- Q&A
- Charts
- Glossaries
- Stand-alone anecdotes

Miami-Dade County Public Schools used this alternative style in 2005, after the area was hit by three hurricanes that closed schools for a number of weeks. One of the many challenges facing the school system was communicating a slew of details surrounding school reopening.

Rather than writing pages of dense prose about procedures and protocols, school system leaders designed the information in a series of short, one-page questions and answers. They selected relevant topics, identified pertinent questions, and wrote concise answers, transforming complex information into easily digestible chunks. The clear presentation of information turned a daunting job into a manageable one. Well-designed information ensures your readers will understand what you want to convey.

AVOID THE CURSE OF KNOWLEDGE

Educators and writers Chip and Dan Heath identify a big barrier to writing effectively: too much knowledge.

What? Weren't we taught that good writing is rooted in knowledge of subject matter? Hold on. The Heath brothers' message, in their best-selling book, *Made to Stick* (2007), is just how difficult it is to explain information on a topic we know well because it's tough to imagine what it's like not to know it. We assume because we know what early childhood education means, everyone else knows it too.

Be concrete. Include details that may seem overly routine or simple to you. Use the details to anchor your readers in your message. Use generalizations and watch their (imaginary) eyes glaze over!

To be an effective school leader turned writer, communicate by putting yourself in the shoes of your readers. Talking to parents about issues before you begin writing will give you valuable insight into what they currently know, what they need to know, and how you can fill the gaps with meaningful information.

WRITE FROM THE HEART

Whether you are writing about the introduction of a new class in Farsi, a change in the cafeteria menu, or new regulations from the central office, find a way to connect with your audience.

- Put a person, real or imagined, in the paragraph. (Describe the possibilities open to a person who graduates speaking Farsi.)
- Set a positive tone. (Add a comment on how the new vegetarian dishes are being received. Yum.)
- Show your own passion. (Even school regulations can stand for things we care about!)

We have said this before, but it is worth repeating: while we work hard to muster all the possible intellectual arguments to support our plans, our projects, and our points of view, in the end people are swayed by how they *feel* about issues. Don't miss the opportunity to write about *what matters*.

EDIT AS IF YOUR LIFE DEPENDED ON IT

Two words about editing: be ruthless.

Writing and rewriting clarifies thinking and purpose. There's no way around it. Simply reading what you've written aloud, even to yourself, will often tell you if your message has clarity and says with passion what you mean to say. Maybe you'll need to go back to the drawing board more than once. Can you outline your key points easily?

One district department we worked with routinely asked three staff members to write the opening paragraph of any important document.

The three spent a lot of time on that one paragraph, each first writing her/his own, then getting together to critique each other's and finally rewriting together. Once the focus had been clarified and that first paragraph was hammered out, the rest of the piece usually came together with relative ease

Asking the stakeholders for whom you're writing can be helpful too. One school system we worked with was preparing an extensive (and expensive) report to be used in a staff development session for principals. We took a couple pages of the report to a few principals and asked for feedback. Would they find this information useful? What points were being made? What suggestions for improvement did they have?

Because we were "outsiders" and promised the principals anonymity, they were honest. Boy, were they honest. But, in the end, the school system was glad they had asked for feedback. By editing the report carefully, they were able to connect effectively with their audience.

AVOID "HAPPY TALK"

Consumers of school information reject articles that are filled with happy talk. Happy talk is content-free, "have a nice day" small talk. While it's perfectly acceptable to interject happy talk in *speaking*, happy talk in *writing* adds unwanted clutter to the printed page. Here's an example:

> Thank you to the many families who participated in Heritage Night. The staff and volunteers put many hours and much thought into making these events special for you and your students. We greatly appreciate that you find time in your busy schedules to join us. We recognize that these are the types of elementary school experiences that students remember for many years. If you have comments or would like to share your thoughts and suggestions about these events, as always, we would appreciate hearing from you.

Every sentence is happy talk—from the thanks, appreciation, and recognition, to the offer for readers to share thoughts and suggestions. Administrators traditionally have turned to the happy talk technique as a tool to be upbeat about what's going on at school. It no longer serves that purpose. Instead, today's reader, who lives in an environment where economy of words is critical, categorizes this kind of communication as spam.

Now, it's very important to thank people and to demonstrate an environment of gratitude, but here are some ways to do so without undermining your message:

- Want to acknowledge a past event? A picture will tell a thousand words.
- Want to thank volunteers? Send them a thank you, acknowledge them personally, create certificates, arrange events for volunteers, etc.
- Want feedback from parents? Offer a simple-to-use feedback card at the event. Each of those solutions provides a connection that happy talk does not.

IF AT FIRST, YOU DON'T SUCCEED

Perhaps the biggest misconception about writing that people have is thinking that you can sit down cold and pound out an effective message or two in the thirty minutes after school dismisses or before the school board meeting. If you can, you should be grateful.

All the successful athletes we know, warm up before a game. Most successful writers warm up too. Write a draft on Monday. Let your brain work on it overnight while you are watching the evening news. Revise the draft on Tuesday. Ask someone to read it for you on Wednesday. Revise again. And, by Thursday or Friday, you should be in good shape.

OK, so the gas main just broke and you have twenty minutes to get out a parent letter. Right. For those occasions, we suggest you build a file of templates that you can modify to fit the occasion. But, for most of your important communication you have lead time. If you need to, build in more lead time—and use it. Start early. It is surprising how much less stressful that makes writing.

We take time with our writing, because it shows respect for our employees, our parents, and our community. We care about our relationships and so we craft our written words carefully. As always in good communication, the return on the time we spend up front well exceeds the investment. Write well.

● ● ●

Writing clearly and convincingly is a process with no simple formulas. Many excellent reference manuals and texts are available for writers that contain nuts and bolts information about grammar, writing mechanics, and techniques to shape content. Simplicity, clarity, and passion are good places for educators to start.

For reflection

1. Look closely at a piece of mail that you didn't open yet destined for the wastebasket. What words led to your rejection?
2. Review a stack of information you've saved for later reading. Pick out those you can admit you'll probably never read. What words clarify your decision not to read?
3. Pick out the most readable piece of paper on your desk. What strategies did the writer use to make it readable?

22

UPGRADE BACK-TO-SCHOOL NIGHT

Curing What Ails This Annual Event

When people know they can rely on each other, when there is a true sense of community, it is amazing how well people perform.

—Margaret Wheatley

In the old days, teachers saw back-to-school night as their opportunity to meet face-to-face with parents of children who misbehaved in class. The hope was that Mom and Dad would go home and make Johnny pay attention.

One problem: Johnny's parents rarely showed up, and teachers were left with the dutiful parents of obedient children waiting to hear what a delight Suzy was to have in class. The morning-after faculty room was filled with consternation, "Why is it that the parents who need to come to back-to-school night, don't?"

Back then, back-to-school night was an annual ritual that established that all was well for the parents who already knew it. A teacher's authority remained unquestioned, and parents who attended generally appreciated the fact that school folks would return to school in the evening to meet with them. Some call those the good old days.

Back-to-school night in the twenty-first century is still an annual affair, but like all rituals it has evolved with the times. Today, it's seen by parents as a fact-finding mission to judge school quality. It provides parents with a snapshot that either reassures or alarms. As generals are tested on the battlefield, school leadership is tested on back-to-school night.

Its success is a measure of the leader's ability to transform an environment created for students to one focused on building relationships with their parents. The stakes are high.

AVOID THE HORROR STORIES

A public address system that doesn't work, a frazzled teacher who complains about his overcrowded classroom, an agenda for the evening that doesn't accommodate smooth transitions between classes combine to form a picture of the school that may not square with what really goes on when children are there. Parents don't want to make that leap of faith. Instead, we must meet parents' expectations and offer them a connection to the school that gives them confidence that this is a well-run school.

One parent was infuriated when a teacher scolded her for leafing through the teacher's handout before being instructed to do so. Another was offended by the length of a teacher's acrylic fingernails. A third grumbled about too many waiting lines. A father scoffs at the dispassionate delivery of curriculum goals and classroom rules—what the teacher regarded as the tangible facts that parents needed to know. All leaped to the same conclusion: lack of competence.

Parents don't need to give up a precious evening at home to get the facts and figures about their child's school. They can find this information elsewhere. Instead, parents come to back-to-school night for assurances. They trust what they see and hear, touch, feel, and smell. How do we use their senses to communicate the school's mission?

IT'S THE RELATIONSHIPS (STUPID)

Political operative James Carville's success in large measure is his insistent focus on a single core message. In managing Bill Clinton's first run for the White House, he advised Clinton to contain his focus to one key message: it's the economy (stupid). It worked. Carville's lesson is clear: one message communicated well gets attention.

The single word for school leaders planning back-to-school night? Relationships. Because children achieve more when the parent and school work together, back-to-school night becomes a kick-off gala to build relationships between home and school. With a successful event, the school is rewarded by increased student achievement. A parent who feels that he's developed a relationship with the school and his child's teacher has taken an important step toward becoming a trusted supporter who gives back to the school anything from tacit permission ("I can see you know what you're doing. Carry on") to an agreement to support from home ("Help me help my child.") to active involvement in school events ("I want to be part of the excitement"). With relationships in place, the length of the teacher's fingernails fades into the background. Pull out all the stops.

Are You Ready for Feedback?

We recently overheard a parent grousing about an event at his son's school. His lack of enthusiasm centered on three missteps: lines, lectures, and lack of options.

"Lines are just a waste of time," he said, saying they signaled a lack of planning on the part of the school. He described sitting in small chairs as the principal walked them through a lot of information that he said could have been included in a flyer. Finally, he found fault with the lack of opportunity to select activities that would allow him to interact on a smaller group level with teachers, administrators, and other parents.

We asked three other parents what they thought about this father's comments:

- "I know that principals aren't trained as event planners, but I would expect a well organized event."
- "My daughter's orientation was terrific. We left feeling we were part of a great school community."
- "I think this father speaks for a lot of parents. Quite frankly, many of us dread attending school events."

Event planning for principals is unlikely ever to be a course requirement for certification, yet many, many school events are planned and executed with flair and attention to the details that insure accomplishment of an important goal—parent involvement. Perhaps looking at school functions as events that require careful and thoughtful planning is a first step toward giving them the attention to detail they require.

TELL MOTIVATING STORIES

Communicate your focus to staff by telling stories. Nordstrom uses stories with great success in training employees to align their actions with the company vision. For example, they recount the tale of a Nordstrom employee who cheerfully agreed to wrap a gift the customer bought at Macy's. The story telegraphs the Nordstrom expectation for customer service. It's simple, easy to remember, and teaches how to manage unique challenges a new employee will face. It communicates in a way that simply saying "Our mission is customer service" does not.

Use a similar strategy to help your staff focus behavior on back-to-school night. Find stories by looking at the event from the parent's point of view. High school parent Joan told us her motivation for attending the event and her strategy for negotiating her daughter's seven classes.

"I wanted teachers to know who I am and that I'm interested in Sheri's education," she said. "I made it a point to give each teacher my business card."

Joan, like many parents, wants to build a relationship with her daughter's teachers. She doesn't want to leave the evening feeling like she's been an anonymous visitor. Many parents we've interviewed say that a major objective in attending is for their child's teachers to take note and conclude that they were good parents. They believe their presence benefits their child.

After we told this story to one principal, she created large, readable nametags with—"My student is . . ." printed on top. She set up a welcome center in the school lobby and handed parents nametags along with a warm greeting. Parents didn't need to be told what to do; they picked up one of the available Sharpies, wrote their child's name and put on the nametag.

"I'd never thought of it from the parent's point of view before," the principal said. "And the name tags were a huge hit with both parents and teachers."

"Since so many parents have different last names from their child's, we decided to have the child's name displayed," the principal said. "We wanted to make things easier for the parent and the teacher to make the connection. In addition, I asked teachers to post large sign-in sheets in each classroom with a list of the students and space after each child for the parent(s) to sign."

This story communicates the importance of parents' expectations and tells how a school can meet them. It says that building a relationship is important to parents and that, when a school takes action, it shows that relationships are equally important to the school as well.

TEACHERS AND PARENT RELATIONSHIPS

Involve teachers in planning the back-to-school-night process by organizing a meeting that provides an opportunity for them to tell stories of their own. Not the horror stories, but ones in which they relate how they handle the unexpected, how they get to know parents, what they do to prepare. Break the event planning down into three stages of the relationship-building process: inviting parents to come, talking to them when they get there, following up with them after the event.

A teacher we know sends personalized invitations to all of her students' parents, and then follows up with e-mails the day after the event. She sends one e-mail to parents who attended and another to those who couldn't attend—not chastising them, but offering another opportunity to connect.

The most challenging part for the teacher is planning what to say and do when coming face-to-face with the parent. The *MetLife Survey of the American Teacher: Transitions and the Role of Supportive Relationships* found that the biggest challenge new teachers face and the areas in which they feel least prepared centers around encouraging and making use of parent involvement (2005). Don't assume teachers know what to do or how to act without leadership and direction. Teachers who are comfortable in front of a class of students report being terrified when confronted with a group of parents.

Rich Bagin, executive director of the National School Public Relations Association encourages teachers to greet parents outside the classroom door, to plan and time their presentation ahead of time, to have a handout, to show enthusiasm, and to make sure parents know you're willing to give extra help (Bagin, 2005).

You can help teachers develop a core message about what goes on in their classroom. The content of the message is important. We're looking for ideas that will stick. A French teacher builds her message on the fact that every student she's ever taught has passed New York State's French regents exam. That remarkable feat is something parents can remember. It's the start of a relationship.

MANAGE THE ENVIRONMENT

At one elementary school, parent Jennifer Jackson's back-to-school night experience led her to conclude that the school was incapable of meeting her daughter's learning needs. Her assessment was based on indicators she interpreted from the environment.

"They had all of the parents crowded into a small room sitting in tiny chairs. It was so hot in there I couldn't breathe," she said. "I don't know how my daughter can learn there."

The school environment is filled with physical signs that lead a parent to an impression of either comfort or distress. We dress for success on the job interview, clean the house for expected guests, and wax the car we're trying to sell. Yet, we forget that such details are critical when our "guests" visit us at school.

When you've lived with a hairstyle for fifteen years, it may take a well-intended friend to whisper that it's time for a change. Ask a trusted parent to help you review the school environment, including such things as signs, parking, and landscaping. Is arriving at your school a pleasant experience?

One school leader addressed the limited parking available for parents by asking her faculty to park at a nearby shopping mall and be bused over to the school. She noted on the evening's program the gesture her staff had made to welcome their guests. Another principal, new to the school in September, enlisted parental help in landscaping the front entrance. A third committed resources to a new school marquee.

Interior environment includes signs, cleanliness, temperature, and other ambient conditions. A predictable first comment in evaluating the evening will refer to the temperature (if it's too warm or cold), the public address system (if there were too many interruptions to classroom discussion), or the restrooms (if they're marked by graffiti or lack soap and paper towels). Don't dismiss these details. They matter.

In an effort to upgrade the appearance of school restrooms, a high school principal asked the officers of school clubs and organizations each to adopt one. Students embraced the challenge and did more than just take responsibility for keeping them clean, but added decorations paint and themes. The science club restroom took on an underwater theme; the student government chose a message of "power to the people"; and the art club brought impressionism to a whole new environment. Their renovations became a source of conversation, pride, and rivalry throughout the year. And the parents at back-to-school night— well, you can imagine the positive comments.

Relationships are the bottom line for a successful back-to-school night. Managing the people, process, and physical dimensions, school leaders can make the most of the opportunity for positive connections. Dedicating up-front time to back-to-school-night planning requires trusting that you will be rewarded down the road. We believe you will. Parents who leave offering you their approval of an evening well spent become your valuable partners in the business of educating children.

• • •

Back-to-school night can be much more than a ho-hum ritual. See it as an opportunity to start a conversation with those partners you need to reach your school's success: increased student achievement. Reenergize this event and focus its outcome on turning disparate parents into trusting members of the school family.

For reflection

1. How can you engage your entire staff in preparations for next year's back-to-school night?
2. List some questions you could ask a parent focus group to gain insight into how to improve parent's back-to-school-night experience. What are some actions your school could take to act on these insights?
3. What are some tactics the school can deploy in the weeks following back-to-school night that will build on the school-home connection?

CONCLUSION

SUSTAINABILITY

The Challenge of the Long-Distance Runner

Back during our prehistory those of us who were able to come to clear conclusions and to act quickly on these conclusions—Are you friend or foe? Do I eat you or do you eat me?—were more likely to survive than those of us who, confused by the world's complexity, dithered and dallied.

—Marcus Buckingham

We were sitting at a small, round conference table—our papers and notebooks spread out before us—trying to organize our thoughts for an upcoming principals' workshop. Meg had created a grid of questions principals might ask themselves and actions they might take to improve communications in their schools.

Kitty pointed to Meg's grid and threw up her hands.

"Your boxes make me crazy! They make me claustrophobic. I need more space to move in." We both laughed.

We had been working for months—with newsprint and markers, drafts and revisions, e-mails and notes—trying to find an effective way to engage school principals and superintendents around the issues of communication leadership. We were trying to synthesize what we had learned over many years with schools and school systems in words that would be compelling to school leaders. We had binders chock full of ideas, but had not found the proper structure in which to put our thoughts. The framework eluded us. That morning we were squabbling over boxes.

"I wish we could use the Lakota circle," mused Meg. (She had just visited the Smithsonian's Museum of the American Indian in Washington, D.C.)

"Oh, terrific," Kitty responded. "I am sure *that* will pique a principal's curiosity!"

Meg elaborated. "The tribe always starts its journey in the east," she said drawing a circle on a clean piece of paper. "So to describe our work, we could write the word 'vision' here."

She wrote *vision* at three o'clock on the circle.

"And here, at six, we could write 'intuition, intention, and skill' because those are the things that will sustain our communication journey. Then we would come around to nine o'clock, to 'relationships,' where the work really takes hold, and finally at the top to 'community' which is the destination."

Meg added the words *student learning*—our goal—in the middle of the circle and wrote *Communication Leadership* at the top of the paper.

There was a long silence as we looked down at what she had drawn. We both recognized in front of us the shape of the framework we had been looking for. All the important words had fallen into place.

We live in too many boxes—especially in our education world. We design organizational charts and financial spreadsheets. We have goals and objectives, missions and strategies.

Boxes have a function. In the best worlds, they give us a foundation from which we can move ourselves and our organizations forward. But boxes can also be static and confining. We use them to isolate ourselves. "It's not in my job description," we say.

Conceptualizing our work as a circle gives us flow, movement. Circles open the possibility of relationships. Circles embrace inclusive and innovative practices.

FINDING THE CORE

Recently, we were part of a support team that helped an elementary principal and the school leadership team (composed of teachers and parents) to develop a new vision and plan for the school. Under the principal's leadership, the team had decided to throw out all the old boxes and look at their mission with fresh eyes. Many of the students in this school belonged to families newly immigrated to this country and this community. English was often not their first language, and many of these families fell well below the poverty line.

During the planning session, the team wrestled to define the core values of the school. It was hard for them to narrow the long list they had created: collaboration, compassion, consistency, constancy, honesty, the home-school connection, children learning from each other.

Finally, the PTA president said quietly, "We want this school to be a second home for our children."

This was the goal that the group had been trying to describe. Now they could flesh out a plan to support their goal. Test scores and accountability loomed large for this community, but the team was willing to throw out the old rubrics and start again with a new, more supple framework—one built on relationships—that offered the school and its stakeholders the possibility of new outcomes.

There are many compelling reasons for principals and schools to rethink and reframe their vision and to reexamine how they communicate within their schools and with their communities. For too long, we have run our schools much as they were run generations ago. The textbooks may be new, but the first-day-of-school rituals remain the same. The gym may have a twenty-first-century climbing wall for students, but we often manage our faculty meetings as we always did. Our high schools may now encourage all students to take Advanced Placement and International Baccalaureate courses, but we respond to parents' questions and complaints with the same arms-length treatment that our own parents received.

It is time for a new story. It is time for us to climb out of our boxes and, together, imagine ways in which schools can be more resilient as we meet the challenges that sit at our doors. We need to think more in circles.

SUSTAINING THE MISSION

"Sustained success means making the greatest possible impact over the longest period of time." So says Marcus Buckingham (2005, p. 224), researcher and author on the subject of leadership. This is the kind of success we want for our students. It's the kind of success we want for ourselves and our schools: *the greatest impact over the longest time.*

Change is not over until it has roots, says John Kotter (2002), by which he means you are not done until you can see new behaviors in your stakeholders. But we keep coming back to the same question: How do you grow those roots? It is one thing to announce a new emphasis on teacher-parent relationships, to hold a back-to-school open house for media reporters, or invite some business leaders to a lunch prepared by the culinary arts students. But how do you engage your community—or communities—in the long-term dialogue that gives your school and district *the greatest possible impact over the longest period of time?*

A good deal has been written for business leaders on the issue of sustainability, and it would be worth our while to borrow some ideas. It might surprise you to find that many of the keys to long-term success are the same as those needed to begin the journey in the first place! Following is a short list of things we need to create sustained, effective communications in our schools:

A vision. We have to be able to paint a picture of what this better life will look like for the people we lead: "If we build strong relationships with each other, we create a supportive environment for our students and for ourselves." That vision can sometimes best be expressed in a symbol or a story: our circles or John Kotter's penguins or the PTA president's vision of the school "as a second home for our students."

We are defined by our stories, which continually form us and make us vital and give us hope.

—Max DuPree

Urgency. The vision must have relevance to all the stakeholders, but there must also be urgency. If this is not a matter that needs to be fixed *now*, you will have trouble mobilizing the troops.

A roadmap. People need to know how you and they will get to the vision. The roadmap must be broken down into small steps and be connected to a reasonable timeframe. If you go to AAA for directions from Washington, D.C., to Charleston, South Carolina, the map not only tells you that the entire trip will be 545 miles, but it also marks the number of miles and the driving time to each town and city along the way.

Flexibility. Our ability to adjust is key to our ability to sustain success. On our trip to Charleston, as we pass Rocky Mount, we might suddenly find ourselves, by mistake, on I40 heading to Wilmington. We will have to adjust our plan and take the coastal route from Wilmington to Charleston.

In today's world, the organization that can adapt is the one that will survive, says Margaret Wheatley (1994), a scientist who studies how organizations grow or die. Leaders, she concludes, must tolerate messiness, support diversity, welcome surprise, expect invention, and rely on the contributions of their best employees.

The ability to recover. In our zest to reach our goals, we often gloss over our mistakes and miss the opportunities those mistakes offer us.

A study of champion tennis players concludes that "what differentiated the best from the rest was not what happened *during* the points, but rather what happened *between* the points." It was about the athletes' ability to recover from each effort (Buckingham, 2005, p. 228).

Research on service recovery (what you do when you make a mistake with your customer) shows that a good recovery effort often brings greater customer loyalty than before (Zeithaml and Bitner, 1996; Barlow and Moeller, 1996).

Both of these kinds of recovery efforts shift our focus. Sometimes the most important action is not what is happening on center stage.

Collaboration. In case we have not made it clear thus far, communication *is* a communal endeavor. We have addressed this book to you, as leader, but communication is everyone's job. You cannot do this work alone. This work is not just about you reaching out. It's about you helping everyone to build new relationships and work collaboratively.

"The lone warrior myth of leadership is a sure route to heroic suicide. Nobody is smart enough or fast enough to engage alone the political complexity of an organization or community when it is facing and reacting to adaptive pressures" (Heifetz, 2002, p. 100).

> The best of breed lead not by virtue of power alone, but by excelling in the art of relationship.
>
> —Daniel Goleman

"To live in a quantum world, we will need to become savvy about how to build relationships, how to nurture growing, evolving things. All of us will need better skills in listening, communicating, and facilitating groups, because these are the talents that build strong relationships" (Wheatley, 1994, p. 38).

Passion. We have already talked about how easy it is for we educators to stay in our heads, but it is when we communicate our passion that we are strong.

"We see, we feel, we change," says John Kotter. It is all about people. What sustains success is our own enthusiasm and creativity and that of the people who work for us (2002).

Educators have passion. Just ask any of them why they stay in the game. It's just that we forget to express it and use its power.

> People get the courage to try new things not because they are convinced to do so by a wealth of analytical evidence but because they feel something viscerally.
>
> —Gary Hamel

Humor. When the going gets tough—and it will—the ability of an organization to laugh can make a huge difference in its ability to rise above the potholes.

"The sound of laughter signals the group's emotional temperature, offering one sure sign that people's hearts as well as their minds are engaged" (Goleman, Boyatzis, and McKee, 2002, p. 11). "If you—and others—aren't having fun doing what you are doing, chances are you're not doing your best" (Kouzes, 2002, p. 198).

The leader's ability to find renewal for his or her own soul. Of all the components of sustainability, this, in the end, may be the most important—and often the least acknowledged. Leading a passionate, engaged organization over time is exhausting. No matter how collegial the work is, the leader bears the most weight. When the leader's energy flags, the organization feels the drag.

Renewal for the leader is a job that only the leader can do for himself or herself.

"The crux of leadership development that works is self-directed learning: intentionally developing or strengthening an aspect of who you are or who you want to be, or both" (Goleman, Boyatzis, and McKee, 2002, p. 109).

How you discover what nourishes you, how you "uncover [your] own dreams and personal ideals, examine [your] strengths" (Goleman, Boyatzis, and McKee, 2002, p. 233) is a journey you undertake on your own. But woe to you and your organization if you don't.

Leader burnout leads to boredom, anxiety, fear, and anger—not just of the leader, but also of staff members, parents, and, eventually, of the students. The downward spiral in a community can be rapid and devastating. We have seen leader burnout morph into parent protests, scorching newspaper editorials, high staff turnover, and city council budget cuts.

RENEWING THE COMMITMENT

Sustained learning occurs in community. We learn best when we are in relationship with others who share a common purpose and a common practice. If schools are indeed to become real learning communities—where adults learn with each other and alongside the students—then the only way to build such communities is by talking with each other. Conversations open possibility and movement. We are talking about circles.

The leader's skill as communicator plays a central role in the sustainability and survival of the organization. Research shows—and our experience confirms—that good communication builds cooperation and teamwork, innovation and creativity. Good communication builds a climate of resiliency. It fosters the enthusiastic support of the community. Good communication undergirds the best teaching and learning.

In many communities across the country, Trader Joe's has become a favorite place to shop. Grocery items on the shelves range from the basic to the unusual. Their prices are among the best in town. Best of all, Trader Joe's has a way of turning a weekly chore into a festive outing.

Writer and columnist Len Lewis took it upon himself to investigate the secrets of TJ's success and wrote a book about what he found (2005). Among the tenants that Trader Joe's management holds dear:

Dare to be different.
Make it fun.
Always deliver value.
Constantly innovate.
Foster a loyal workforce.
Ignite the imagination.
Make it adaptable.
Build a brand with a human touch.

These are Trader Joe's tools for creating *the greatest impact over the longest time*. We in schools could do worse than to follow their lead.

REFERENCES

Allen, J. (2007). *Social Media Drove "Jena Six" into National Spotlight*. Retrieved January 31, 2008 from http://www.ragan.com.

Associated Press. (2008). "Teacher Absences Are Hurting Learning: Vacuum in Classroom Linked to Lower Test Scores, Research Shows," January 16.

Bagin, R., ed. (2007a). *School Public Relations: Building Confidence in Education*. Rockville, MD: National School Public Relations Association (NSPRA).

Bagin, R., ed. (2007b). *How Strong Communications Help Superintendents Get and Keep Their Jobs: A Study to Identify the Qualities Desired in Superintendents*. Rockville, MD: National School Public Relations Association (NSPRA).

Bagin, R., ed. (2007c). *Voices on the Front Line: Superintendents Talk about the Value of School Communication*. Rockville, MD: National School Public Relations Associates (NSPRA).

Bagin, R., ed. (2005). "Make the Most of Your Back-to-School Night Presentation." In *Principal Communicator*. Rockville, MD: National School Public Relations Association (NSPRA).

Barlow, J., and Moeller, C. (1996). *A Complaint Is a Gift*. San Francisco: Berrett-Koehler Publishers.

Buckingham, M. (2005). *The One Thing You Need to Know . . . About Great Managing, Great Leading, and Sustained Individual Success*. New York: Free Press.

Bulach, C., Boothe, D., and Pickett, W. (1998). "The Impact of Human Relations Training on Levels of Opinion and Trust." *Research for Educational Reform* 8(4): 43–57.

Carr, N., APR (2005). "The Evidence Is Clear: It Pays for Public Schools to Spend More on Communications." *NSPRA Counselor*. National School Public Relations Association (NSPRA) (March).

Carr, N., APR (2007). "Marketing Your Schools." In *School Public Relations: Building Confidence in Education*, ed. Rich Bagin, (pp. 209–28). Rockville, Maryland: National School Public Relations Association (NSPRA).

Cary, A. (2006). *How Strong Communication Contributes to Student and School Success: Parent and Family Involvement*. Rockville MD: National School Public Relations Association (NSPRA), 6–7.

Carville, J., and Begala, P. (2002). *Buck Up, Suck Up . . . and Come Back When You Foul Up. 12 Winning Secrets From the War Room*. New York: Simon and Schuster.

Collins, J. (2001). *Good to Great: Why Some Companies Make the Leap . . . and Others Don't*. New York: Harper Business.

Covey, S. (2006). *The Speed of Trust*. New York: Free Press.

Davis, S. H. (1998). "Why Do Principles Get Fired?" *Principal* 28(2): 34–39.

Fullan, M. (2001). *Leading in a Culture of Change*. San Francisco: Jossey Bass.

Garmston, R., and Wellman, B. (1999). *The Adaptive School: A Sourcebook for Developing Collaborative Groups*. Norwood, MA: Christopher-Gordon Publishers.

Goleman, D. (1998). *Working with Emotional Intelligence*. New York: Bantam Books.

Goleman, D., Boyatzis, R., and McKee, A. (2002). *Primal Leadership: Realizing the Power of Emotional Intelligence*. Boston: Harvard Business School Press.

Grunig, J., ed. (2002). *Excellence in Pubic Relations and Communication Management*. Mahwah, NJ: Lawrence Erlbaum Associates.

Grunig, J. (2006). "Furnishing the Edifice: Ongoing Research on Public Relations as a Strategic Management Function." *Journal of Public Relations Research* 18(2): 151–76.

Hallowell, E. M. (1999). *Connect*. New York: Pocket Books.

Heath, C., and Heath, D. (2007). *Made to Stick: Why Some Ideas Survive and Others Die*. New York: Random House.

Henderson, A., and Mapp, K. (2002). *A New Wave of Evidence: The Impact of School, Family and Community Connections on Student Achievement*. Austin, TX: Southwest Education Development Lab.

Heifetz, R., and Linsky, M. (2002). *Leadership on the Line: Staying Alive through the Dangers of Leading*. Boston: Harvard Business School Press.

Howe, N., and Strauss, W. (2007). "The Next 20 Years: How Customers and Workforce Attitudes Will Evolve." *Harvard Business Review* (July).

Hunter, B. (2005). *Promoting Public Schools and Discussing Federal Issues: A Blueprint for School System Leaders* (presentation). Arlington, VA: American Association of School Administrators.

Jackson, P. (1994). "Evalution of PR Vital, but Not Being Done." *PR Reporter* 37(50).

Jaworski, J. (1996). *Synchronicity: The Inner Path of Leadership,* San Francisco: Berrett-Koehler Publishers, Inc.

Ketcham and University of Southern California Annenberg Strategic Public Relations Center (2008). "Media Myths and Realities: a Pubic of One." *Perspectives.* Ketchum's Online Magazine. Retrieved January 31, 2008, from http://www.ketchumperspectives.com/archives/2008_i1/jan2008issue.php.

Kochanek, J. R. (2005). *Building Trust for Better Schools.* Thousand Oaks, CA: Corwin Press.

Kotter, J. (1996). *Leading Change.* Boston: Harvard Business School Press.

Kotter, J. (2002). *The Heart of Change.* Boston: Harvard Business School Press.

Kouzes, J., and Posner, B. (2002). *The Leadership Challenge.* San Francisco: Jossey-Bass.

Kowalski, T., Petersen, G., and Fusarelli, L. (2007). *Effective Communication for School Administrators.* Lanham, MD: Roman & Littlefield Education.

Kugler, E. (2002). *Debunking the Middle-Class Myth: Why Diverse Schools Are Good for All Kids.* Lanham MD: Scarecrow Press, Inc.

Laun, C. (2007). "Scientific Web Design: 23 Actionable Lessons from Eye-Tracking Studies." Retrieved January 31, 2008, from http://www.virtualhosting.com/blog/2007/scientific-web-design-23-actionable-lessons-from-eye-tracking-studies/.

Lazenby, R., ed. (2007). *April 16: Virginia Tech Remembers.* New York: Penguin.

Lewis, L. (2005). *The Trader Joe's Adventure.* Chicago: Dearborn Publishing.

Matthews, D. (2002). "Why Principals Fail—and What We Can Learn from It." *Principal* 82(1): 38–40.

McCarthy, C. (n.d.)."I'd Rather Teach Peace." NPR broadcast, Humanmedia.org, program #85, 86.

Mehrabian, Dr. A. (1981). *Silent Messages: Implicit Communication of Emotion and Attitudes.* Belmont, CA: Wadsworth.

MetLife Foundation (2005). *The MetLife Survey of the American Teacher.* Retrieved January 31, 2008, from http://www.metlife.com/Applications/Corporate /WPS/CDA/PageGenerator/0,4773,P2817,00.html.

Pearson, C., and Porath, C. (2005). "On the Nature, Consequences and Remedies of Workplace Incivility: No Time for 'Nice'? Think Again." *Academy of Management Executive* 19(1): 7–18.

Pew Internet and American Life Project (2007). "Teens and Social Media." Retrieved January 31, 2008, from http://pewinternet.org/pdfs/PIP_Teens _Social_Media_Final.pdf.

Rudick, M., and O'Flahavan, L. (2002). *Clear, Correct, Concise E-Mail: A Writing Workbook for Customer Service Agents*. Silver Spring, MD: E-Write.

Salacuse, J. (2006). *Leading Leaders: How to Manage Smart, Talented, Rich, and Powerful People*. New York: American Management Association.

Senge, P., Kleiner, A., Roberts, C., Ross, R., Roth, G., and Smith, B. (1999). *The Dance of Change: The Challenges to Sustaining Momentum in Learning Organizations*. New York: Currency Doubleday.

Stanford, J. (1999). *Victory in Our Schools: We Can Give Our Children Excellent Public Education*. New York: Bantam Books.

Susskind, L., and Field, P. (1996). *Dealing with an Angry Public: The Mutual Gains Approach to Resolving Disputes*. New York: Free Press.

Sutton, R. (2007). "Building the Civilized Workplace." *The McKinsey Quarterly* (May).

Vedantam, S. (2007). "Go for It on Fourth Down, Coach? Maybe You Should Ask an Egghead." *Washington Post*, November 5, A3.

Wheatley, M. (1994). *Leadership and the New Science: Learning about Organization from an Orderly Universe*. San Francisco: Berrett-Koehler Publishers, Inc.

Wheatley, M. (2005). *Finding Our Way: Leadership for an Uncertain Time*. San Francisco: Berrett-Koehler Publishers, Inc.

Wukovitz, J. (2006). *Eisenhower: A Biography*. New York: Palgrave Macmillan.

Zeithaml, V., and Bitner, M. (1996). *Services Marketing*. New York: McGraw Hill Companies, Inc.

INTERNET RESOURCES

Office of Safe and Drug-Free Schools, U.S. Department of Education, http://www.ed.gov/admins/lead/safety/schoolsafety/index.html

Fairfax County Public Schools http://www.fcps.edu

Fairfax County Public Schools http://www.fcps.edu/emergencyplan/index.htm

Montgomery County Public Schools
http://www.montgomeryschoolsmd.org/info/emergency/preparedness/

National Association of School Psychologists
http://www.nasponline.org/resources/crisis_safety/index.aspx

Peel District School Board
http://www.peelschools.org

INDEX

24-hour news cycle, 176
9/11, 147, 164

academic standards, 131
accountability, 60, 82, 86, 230
active involvement, 223
active listening, 184
Adequate Yearly Progress, 94
administrative assistants, 136, 142
administrative team, 35, 75
Advanced Placement, 230
advisory panels, 147
Aesop, 21
AIDS, 21
Alexandria Gazette, 100
Alexandria, Virginia, 95, 130
Allen, George, 32
American Life Project, 207
American Red Cross, 101
angry parents, 137
anxiety, 79, 136, 234
Arlington County (Virginia), 129

assistant principal, 2, 8, 30
Associated Press of Virginia, 169
athletic schedules, 166
ATM machine, 195
attendance clerk, 118
attention span, 199
authenticity, 190, 193, 194

back-to-school night, 7, 53, 145, 221,
    222, 223, 224, 226, 227
bacterial meningitis, 163
Bagin, Rich, 225
Barlow, Janelle, 135
Bayer Aspirin, 68
Begala, Paul, 36
bell schedule, 35
benchmarks, 27, 86, 88, 94
bite, snack, and meal, 200
block scheduling, 39
blog, 205, 206, 208, 211, 215
blogosphere, 204
boilerplate responses, 38

bomb threat, 9, 103
bond referendum, 3, 87, 93, 145
book challenges, 146
boomers, 46
boundary changes, 127
Bowman, Robert, 172
branding, 6, 49, 106
breaking news, 123
brochure, 7, 21, 64, 149, 186
Buckingham, Marcus, 228, 230
bulletin boards, 77, 130
bullying, 37
bumper stickers, 68
burnout, 79, 234
business, 1, 2, 3, 7, 14, 15, 16, 53, 73,
    78, 83, 88, 97, 100, 101, 113, 127,
    134, 135, 145, 149, 150, 151, 159,
    195, 196, 207, 224, 227, 231
business card, 224

cable television, 95
cafeteria, 6, 9, 29, 67, 77, 89, 98, 105,
    217
calendar, 149, 191, 215
capital improvement program, 3
Carr, Nora, 3
Carville, James, 36, 222
cell phone, 13, 16, 113, 127, 164,
    171, 175, 177, 208
Center for Teaching Peace, 143
chain of command, 160
Chamber of Commerce, 21, 23, 99
change, 8, 13, 15, 18, 24, 35, 39, 40,
    49, 52, 55, 68, 71, 81, 84, 86, 88,
    89, 90, 93, 96, 98, 99, 102, 113,
    124, 125, 126, 127, 128, 129, 138,
    139, 141, 147, 148, 184, 185, 193,
    202, 217, 226, 233
Churchill, Winston, 21
Citigroup, 101
citizen journalism, 205

city council, 35, 101, 234
clarity, 46, 104, 201, 214, 217, 220
Clear Creek ISD, 209
climate, 3, 5, 8, 29, 78, 85, 89, 96,
    234
Clinton, Bill, 222
coach, 6, 37, 116, 126, 137
coaching skills, 17
collaboration, 43, 48, 49, 51, 80, 198,
    230
Collins, Jim, 2, 39, 94
common vision, 201
communication: audit, 85, 86;
    between home and school, 54;
    breakdown, 186; channels, 197;
    crisis, 159, 160, 163, 167, 175,
    178; daily, 181, 182, 187, 188;
    effective, 8, 173, 231; gap, 187,
    196, 203; intentional, 187;
    interpersonal, 4, 5; lack of, 5, 75,
    197; procedures, 184;
    transparency, 165, 211; team, 115,
    160, 165, 173; techniques, 47
community relations, 2, 160
community: collaboration, 48; dialog,
    55; participation, 48
complaints, 22, 54, 78, 134, 135, 136,
    138, 144, 193, 230
compliments, 29
concrete message, 31
contact information, 120, 198
controversial issues, 196
core message, 222, 225
core values, 208, 230
counselors, 143, 162
creativity, 36, 37, 43, 83, 85, 159,
    171, 233, 234
credibility, 4, 82, 85, 105
Crew, Rudy, 49
crisis: intervention and support, 160;
    management, 105, 159, 160, 167

critical incident, 102, 159, 160, 162, 164, 173, 178
cultural competence, 129, 132
cultural, differences, 132
curriculum, 6, 114, 181, 201, 209, 222
Custom Chucks, 15
custom solutions, 42, 43
customer experience, full, 15
customer, satisfaction, 14
customer service, 1, 8, 14, 45, 71, 77, 81, 138, 182, 224

D-Day invasion, 76
decision-making skills, 171
Delaware State University, 177
delivery system, 65, 69
demanding parent, 49
demographics, 47, 85, 126, 203, 209
disinformation, 93, 204, 209
distrust, 26, 30, 43, 116
diversity, 124, 125, 127, 129, 130, 131, 232
Donne, John, 195
Dover Air Force Base, 21
drive-by shooting, 6
drugs, 154

early adopters, 127
Economic Development Authority, 101
editor, headline, 115
editorial, 208
Edsel, 83
Education Week, 114
elected officials, 7, 64, 66, 108, 146, 198
elevator speech, 107
e-mail, 15, 22, 36, 37, 38, 39, 40, 41, 42, 44, 54, 63, 65, 68, 77, 78, 87, 88, 105, 107, 153, 165, 166, 175, 176, 202, 228

employee, relations, 2, 74
engagement, 48, 50, 51, 52, 53, 187, 205
engaging the community, 25
English as a Second Language, 124
evaluation, 61, 83, 86, 88, 90
event planner, 223
eye contact, 30, 73, 121

Facebook, 22, 175, 177, 206, 210
facilitator, 54
facilities use agreement, 146
fact-finding mission, 222
faculty arrests, 9
faculty meetings, 20, 65, 77, 88, 107, 230
Fairfax County Public Schools, 32, 67, 71, 75, 101, 120, 165, 209
family life education, 146
FBI, 172
Federal Transportation Safety Board, 172
feedback, 17, 53, 76, 83, 89, 143, 185, 206, 213, 218, 219
FERPA, 174
field trip, 20, 186, 195
file sharing, 206
first generation Americans, 14
flexibility, 71, 159
Flickr, 206
focus group, 43, 45, 54, 89, 191
free or reduced-price meals, 125
front line employees, 73
front office, 29, 43, 45, 77, 87, 89, 104, 126, 130, 194, 199
Fullan, Michael, 128

gangs, 146
Garmston, Robert, 19
gatekeepers, 205
GEICO, 106

Geller, Corrine, 172
Generation X, 14, 41, 42, 43, 47, 74
Giuliani, Rudy, 164
Goleman, Daniel, 17, 148, 154, 232
Google, 204, 205, 207
grading system, 87
graphics, 192, 198, 199
grass roots, 34, 127
guidance department, 197

Halloween, 140, 141
Hallowell, Edward M., 28
HAZMAT, 161, 166
Hincker, Larry, 171
Hockett, Steve, 205
Holt, Lester, 177
Home Depot, 200
home-school connection, 230
hostage, 165
human behavior, 135
human relations, 5
human resources, department of, 82
humor, 98, 194
hurricane, 161

illegal immigration, 146
incivility, 77, 78, 79, 80, 142
info-highway, 195
informational meetings, 154
instructional assistant, 72
instructional program, 64, 65, 82, 87
integrity, 9, 25, 26, 27, 32, 33, 102
interactive process, 51
International Baccalaureate, 230
Internet, 14, 16, 32, 37, 41, 44, 45,
     89, 113, 177, 199, 204, 207
interview, 116, 117, 118, 119, 120,
     121, 122, 176, 182, 226

Jackson, Pat, 87
jargon, 7, 193, 198, 213

Jena Six, 204
justice, 137

Kahane, Adam, 18
key communicators, 68, 107, 153
kick-off gala, 223
kindergarten registration, 44
Kotter, John, 17, 231, 233
Kugler, Eileen, 130
Kurtz, Jill, 204

Lakota circle, 229
Lamont, Ned, 34, 35, 39, 147
landscaping, 226
latch-key children, 182
Latino community, 64
lawyers, 173
Lazenby, Roland, 175
Leaders, effective, 154, 160,
     190
learning communities, 6, 234
Lieberman, Senator Joe, 34
Lindberg, Denise, 150
Link, Sylvia, 128
LinkedIn, 206, 210
listening, 18, 19, 24, 27, 35, 53, 54,
     55, 72, 80, 89, 97, 129, 134, 135,
     137, 143, 184, 185, 186, 187, 201,
     233
listening, investment in, 185
listserv, 202
Little League, 196
lock-down, 9, 160, 161
logos, 69

maccaca, 32
Mancusi, Joseph, 18
marketing, 3, 4, 71, 72, 81, 82, 86,
     102, 103, 104, 105, 106, 107, 108,
     109, 148, 149, 152
Mathews, Jay, 113, 114

McCarthy, Coleman, 143
media, relations, 2, 117
mediation, 142, 143
Microsoft, 88, 100
Middle Eastern, 147
minority students, 127
Moeller, Claus, 135
Murrow, Edward R., 181
Museum of the American Indian, 229
Muslim clerics, 147
Mustang, 83
Myanmar, 177
MySpace, 175, 177, 206

nametags, 224
National Honor Society, 31
National School Public Relations Association, 5, 86, 201, 225
Native Americans, 135
NBC, 148, 171
negative feedback, 135
negotiation, 131, 140
neighborhood, blogs, 153
neighborhood, meetings, 35
New York Times, 100
newsletters, 7, 42, 53, 65, 68, 189, 191, 193, 201, 202
No Child Left Behind, 19, 82, 94
Nordstrom, 14, 224
Normandy, 76
Norris Hall, 175, 176, 236
Northern Virginia Association of Realtors, 151

O'Flahavan, Leslie, 200
obesity, 104, 154
Olympics, 15
online, technologies, 206
Ontario, Canada, 128
op-ed piece, 101

parent advisory, committee, 51, 153
parent, focus group, 44, 227
parent-teacher conference, 30
parking, 29, 104, 107, 159, 162, 164, 226
partnership, 43, 48
Pepperdine University, 177
persuasion, 34, 38, 39, 76
Peters, Tom, 59, 104
Pew Internet, 207
photo sharing, 201, 206
podcasts, 207, 209
police incident, 118
polls, 93
post-secondary education, 130, 152
press, open house, 114
principal, 2, 4, 5, 6, 9, 15, 19, 20, 22, 23, 27, 28, 29, 30, 34, 35, 37, 38, 41, 45, 46, 51, 54, 63, 66, 72, 73, 74, 76, 84, 89, 92, 116, 117, 122, 127, 131, 134, 137, 140, 141, 147, 153, 162, 163, 164, 166, 167, 181, 183, 184, 185, 191, 193, 199, 205, 223, 224, 226, 229, 230
psychologists, 143, 162
PTA: fundraiser, 38; meetings, 14, 125, 148; president, 39, 230, 231
public awareness campaign, 126
public relations, 2, 3, 60, 86, 105

radio, 117, 123, 206
real estate agents, 198
recreation department, 145, 154
relationship, development, 183
relationship-building messages, 193
relationships, 42, 90, 114, 183, 222, 223, 225, 227
religious leaders, 64
Remember the Titans, 95, 130
reputation, 33, 101, 102, 104, 108, 181, 196

research, 18, 52, 61, 64, 73, 79, 83, 85, 87, 98, 141, 147

response, 24, 29, 36, 52, 53, 73, 76, 88, 89, 99, 123, 138, 142, 144, 155, 161, 162, 164, 196, 208, 210

right to privacy, 208

risk, 7, 20, 24, 53, 54, 84, 98, 193, 208

Ritz-Carlton Hotels, 138

Roach, Max, 94

Romer, David, 20

Rordam, Ron, 169

Rucker, James, 204

Salacuse, Jeswald W., 2

school board, 5, 6, 9, 17, 22, 50, 52, 53, 66, 67, 72, 75, 85, 91, 99, 134, 136, 146, 163, 165, 219

school: culture, 132; delay of, 123; evacuation of, 160; grapevine, 196

Seattle Public Schools, 97

Senge, Peter, 17

senior citizens, 64, 147

sexual abuse, 159

shelter-in-place, 23, 160

Sidran, Ben, 94

snail mail, 44

snipers, 165

snow days, 103, 150

social media, 113, 175, 177, 202, 204, 205, 206, 207, 208, 209, 211

social networking, 207, 211

social workers, 162

special education services, 104

spokesperson, 64, 174

sponsors, 107

staff development, 49, 129, 218

staff survey, 184

staffing, 108, 134

stakeholder, expectations of, 69

Stanford, Major General John, 97

state department of education, 161

state legislation, 127

stories, 2, 3, 6, 7, 8, 21, 22, 24, 59, 69, 76, 77, 89, 98, 105, 116, 117, 120, 123, 125, 129, 136, 165, 170, 175, 176, 213, 214, 216, 224, 225, 231

strategic, goals, 75

stress, 26, 43, 78, 79, 145, 160, 162, 166

student achievement, 5, 43, 75, 79, 129, 181, 223, 227

student counterfeit ring, 9

student privacy, 118

student-parent reunification, 160

suicide, 161, 172, 232

superintendent, 1, 2, 4, 5, 6, 8, 9, 20, 23, 32, 34, 36, 37, 38, 39, 49, 55, 60, 64, 71, 72, 74, 77, 84, 92, 95, 96, 97, 103, 107, 114, 115, 127, 128, 134, 136, 140, 141, 147, 151, 153, 163, 166, 181, 183, 187, 193

survey, 35, 48, 49, 53, 64, 201, 207

sustainability, 231, 233, 234

systemic change, 127

table-top training, 161

tactics, 66, 67, 68, 107, 142, 153, 227

talk radio, 122

talking points, 116, 163

tangibles, 103

taxpayers, 7, 101, 146

teachable moment, 208

teamwork, 75, 131, 234

technology, 18, 36, 39, 40, 68, 77, 78, 88, 166, 176, 178, 182, 198, 202, 203

telephone tree, 122

television, 105, 115, 121, 123, 131, 159, 164, 166, 176, 177, 206

testing irregularity, 89

text messages, 42
Thurber, James, 20
timeline, 60, 174, 197
toilet paper, 122
top-down management, 182
tornado, 114, 159
town meeting, 77
Trader Joe's, 234, 235
transfer options, 94
trust, 5, 23, 25, 26, 27, 28, 29, 30, 31,
    32, 33, 35, 50, 71, 74, 85, 97, 102,
    104, 122, 126, 138, 147, 187, 222
turnover, high staff, 234
two-way dialogue, 53

UCLA, 121
United Way, 101
USA Today, 192, 216
U.S. Department of Education, 161,
    205
USPS, 15

violence, 154
Virginia Tech, 166, 169, 170, 171,
    172, 174, 176, 177, 236
virtual community, 203
vision, 5, 25, 32, 34, 45, 50, 51, 60,
    61, 71, 74, 75, 93, 94, 117, 126,

132, 148, 184, 186, 213, 224, 229,
    230, 231

Wal-Mart, 100
Washington Post, 21, 100, 113, 114,
    143, 149
Washington, D.C., 130, 165, 229,
    231
Web 2.0, 205
website, 7, 44, 46, 63, 67, 68, 94, 102,
    104, 107, 151, 152, 165, 166, 175,
    176, 195, 196, 197, 198, 199, 200,
    201, 202, 203, 206
Wheatley, Margaret J., 70, 74, 82,
    91
White House, 222
Wiki, 206
Wikipedia, 206
working mom, 195
World War II, 76
Wukovitz, John, 70

year-round school program, 116

Zuch, David, 22
Zappos.com, 14
Zeithaml, Valarie, 73
zero-tolerance, 80

ABOUT THE AUTHORS

Kitty Porterfield directed public relations and communications efforts in public school districts in Northern Virginia for nearly thirty years, most recently in Fairfax County Public Schools, the twelfth-largest school district in the country. She led the communications efforts of Fairfax County schools during 9/11 and the sniper incident in the Washington metropolitan area. Her work has received numerous awards, including recognition from the U.S. Departments of Education and Homeland Security. She is also the recipient of many regional and national awards from the National School Public Relations Association, including the 2004 Gold Medallion and the 2007 Mariner Award for Exceptional Leadership. She lives in Northern Virginia and is a principal in the firm of Porterfield & Carnes Communications. (www.porterfield andcarnes.com). Kitty is currently working on a book about her life as the older sister of a child with multiple disabilities. She can be reached at kitty@porterfieldandcarnes.com.

Meg Carnes has wide-ranging experience in K–12 education as a teacher and administrator. She worked as a communications specialist for Fairfax County (VA) Public Schools when the school division was awarded the Gold Medallion for communication excellence from the

National School Public Relations Association. Previously she was an award-winning journalism teacher. She received the APR (Accreditation in Public Relations) in 2004. Recent published articles include: "Communicating with Generation X," "School Events, Reputation Builders or Breakers," "Use Your Vision to Communicate," and "Make It a Star Spangled Week for Education." She's a frequent presenter at National School Public Relations Association conferences and has served on judging panels for national communications competitions. Meg lives in Washington, D.C., and is a principal in the firm of Porterfield & Carnes Communications (www.porterfieldandcarnes.com). Meg is involved in the local community and competes in 10k running events. She can be reached at meg@porterfieldandcarnes.com.